D0732413

Men's Women's
Business Business

Men's Women's
Business Business

THE SPIRITUAL ROLE OF GENDER IN
THE WORLD'S OLDEST CULTURE

Hannah Rachel Bell

INNER TRADITIONS
ROCHESTER, VERMONT

Inner Traditions International
One Park Street
Rochester, Vermont 05767
www.InnerTraditions.com

Copyright © 1998 by Hannah Rachel Bell

All rights reserved. No part of this book may be reproduced or utilized in any form or by any means, electronic or mechanical, including photocopying, recording, or by any information storage and retrieval system, without permission in writing from the publisher.

LIBRARY OF CONGRESS CATALOGING-IN-PUBLICATION DATA

Bell, Hannah Rachel.
Men's business, women's business : the spiritual role of gender in the world's oldest culture / Hannah Rachel Bell.
p. cm.
ISBN 0-89281-655-4 (pbk. : alk. paper)
1. Philosophy, Ngarinyin.   2. Ngarinyin (Australian people)—Kinship.   3. Ngarinyin (Australian people)—Rites and ceremonies.   4. Sex role—Australia—Kimberley (W.A.)   5. Sexual division of labor—Australia—Kimberley (W.A.)   6. Kimberley (W.A.)—Social life and customs.   I. Title
DU125.N47B45 1998
305.3'09941'4—dc21   98-30380
CIP

Printed and bound in Canada

10 9 8 7 6 5 4 3 2 1

Text design and layout by Bill Brilmayer
This book was typeset in Garamond

Kevin Shaw

To the memory of David Mowaljarlai, without whose friend-ship, inspiration, and wisdom I might never have known that while I write with my right hand, my left hand gives me balance, support, and lift to dance a two-handed life.

MAR - 7 2001

MAR 1991

Table of Contents

Acknowledgments

Thanks to:

Ngarinyin Elders and Friends:
 Mowaljarlai, visionary Lawman, collaborator, and friend. Paddy Neowarra, chairman of Kamali Council and the Ngarinyin Aboriginal Corporation, senior Lawman, mentor, and friend. Laurie Cowanulli, senior Lawman, mentor, and friend. Maisie Nenowatt, Susan Collier, Sandra Mungulu, Jillian Bangmorra, Chloe Nulgitt, and Jacky Dann.

Ngarinyin Children:
 Claude and Gideon Mowaljarlai and their nephew Lukie Mowaljarlai, my "sons." Kane Nenowatt, Clinton Bangmorra, Aaron Mungulu, Deidre Mungulu, Sherika Nulgitt, Deanne Bidd, Danielle Bangmorra, and Naomi, Neil, Neala, and Marvis Maru.

Education Initiative:
 Joan Butun, the Most Reverend Dr. Peter Carnley, archbishop of Perth, Mr. John Moody, Mr. Kim Walton, Mr. Robert Armstrong, Mr.

Allan Meney, Mr. Matthew Hughes, Mrs. Lynne Thompson, Mrs. Audrey Jackson, Mr. Andrew Davidson, Mr. Phil Jurejvich, Mr. John Moore, Father David Thornton-Wakeford, Gabrielle Morrissey, Kathy Charlesworth, and my daughter Jesse Wiles.

Ngarinyin House:
Isobel Peters, a Worrora woman who helped establish and run the home base for the children attending schools in Perth.

Bush University:
Susan Bradley, who has worked with me in many areas of the Ngarinyin Initiative and supported me through many difficult times and challenges. Graeme and Judy Carbury, whose Wedgetail OKA four-wheel drive and mobile infrastructure has made Bush University so successful. Sandy Macken, Jim Macken, Janet Ryan, the Gibb River Community, the Mt. Barnett Community, and Russell and Peta Timms.

Land and Wandjina Foundation:
Tony Coote, David Bradley, Christina and Trevor Kennedy, Alec and Lorraine Shand, Tony Redmond, Diana McCarthy, Bernice Murphy, and Geoffrey Cousins.

Publications, Art, and Film:
Jeff Doring and the Pathways Project, Jutta Malnic, whose friendship and collaboration with Mowaljarlai and me has been deeply sustaining, Peter Collins, Heather Winter, Kirsty Cockburn, George Negus, Suzanna Lobez, Patricia Hamilton, Di Morrissey, Andrew MacFarlane, Peter Harrison, and Tom Spender.

Other Friends:
Father Frank Brennan S.J., Bishop David Murray, Matthew Shand, Susan Sawday, Maureen Babe, Denise Meyer, Greg Pratt, Margaret Gibson, and Susan Hunt.

Jutta Malnic

Lawwoman Susan Collier with Hannah Rachel Bell at Marunbabidi.

The Formation of Identity

I grew up in a family of males. There was my mother, of course, but she was generally invisible to us; only her absence was really noticed. She cooked, cleaned, ironed, gardened, attended school sports, joined the roster of the school canteen, took us to our medical appointments, went to Mother's Union meetings at the local church, and bore more sons. Occasionally she would reluctantly pull out her album of newspaper clippings which contained stories about her triumphs as a national swimmer, a diver, a skilled artist and draftswoman. Or she would take out her photograph album which showed us that she was a real person with a childhood, parents, and a great sense of humor.

As a family, we were far more familiar with my father's life. He grew up in the Torres Strait Islands with the "Islander Natives," the errant son of an enlightened missionary. His was a childhood filled with adventure and the exotic. We loved those wondrous times in the heart of winter when we gathered on the floor in front of the lounge-room fire to listen to our father spin his action-packed tales of riding on the back of a shark, thumbs firmly pressed into its eyes to save himself from being eaten, or stealing cigarette butts from sailors and vagrants and diving for pearls with the natives off the sides of the missionary lugger or from their community boats. As he wove us into his childhood world, mother washed the dishes, heated the milk for the hot chocolate she would carry in on a tray with toasted raisin bread for all of us, and stoked the slow-combustion stove before she shut it down for the night, ensuring us a warm, cozy kitchen when we woke up in the morning. We didn't notice her.

Although I do not remember doing it consciously, at some point in my childhood I must have decided that I would not be an invisible female like my mother. At an early age, I set about being an outstanding athlete like my mother, a storyteller like my father, a public speaker and teacher like my preacher grandfather, a writer like my grandmother, and a politician, healer, artist, actor, activist, missionary, or anything else that would ensure I was somebody with a message, someone who counted. These youthful experiences metamorphosed into full-blown professions later in my life, but when I was a teenager they were statements or intentions.

My father must have known that being a traditional homemaker would not suit me, that I was a rebel like him, constantly challenging the constraints of convention. Each summer holiday, he and my mother sent me away to friends or relations to spend the six-week vacation experiencing their lives. I holidayed in the poverty and hardship of a Soldiers Settlement farm, served customers in a little village general store, camped on the beach with an eccentric psychiatrist and his family, luxuriated in the material pleasures enjoyed by our wealthy cousins, and occasionally stayed with my own family at my grandmother's seaside cottage where we fished, climbed cliffs, spied on lovers in the sand dunes, and played strategy board games. Thinking I must have been too disruptive for the rest of the family if I stayed at home, I once asked my father how come I was the only one of his children whom he sent away. He told me that no matter what I did in my life, I would have to do it better than men because, whether he agreed with it or not, that was the way of the world. He wanted to give me the world.

My being a girl seemed to flummox my father somewhat, but he spent a lot of time engaging me in intellectual and religious challenges and discussions. Perhaps I was the only one of his children who thought the machinations of his mind were such fun; I also thought it was the best way to be visible to him. In any event I enjoyed these private times immensely, always stretching to meet the challenges he wanted me to think about. Being a tomboy opened up other vistas as well. I was able to compete with the boys in their little man's world of strategy, intrigue, and vigor. I learned to fight fiercely, swear outrageously, connive cleverly, wield a wrench and axe competently, push a lawn mower, and play cowboys and Indians or cops and robbers without dying while my mother watched me through the kitchen window as she prepared yet another meal *without* the help of her only daughter. From my teenage years until well into adulthood, my mother implored, "Why can't you just be a normal girl/woman?" How terribly sad she must have been to realize that rather than growing up to share the joys of womanhood with her, I steadfastly turned my back and went outside to join the "real world" where boys were mean and men were tough.

In this world of the 1950s gender was predictable and accepted. Men did particular things and women did other particular things. These things were rarely challenged, the boundaries of responsibility seldom breached. Women's Business for Western women meant that mothers had babies, looked after homes and families, did volunteer work and homecrafts. Men's Business generally meant that fathers went *out* to work, earned money, and held the dominant positions in family, community, and the nation. Fathers were obviously and emphatically very important. They had power, influence, and authority over the whole world. It was certainly my experience that men made all the decisions about everything that I knew to be significant in my life.

Like all teenagers I was quite impressionable, and noted that the things that men did attracted great recognition. Like millions of females at my age and stage of life in the 1950s, I was guided, even coerced by schoolteachers, ministers, and many other significant adults into assuming the roles and functions that my culture had fashioned for me. But like many other emerging young women, I reached the infamous 1960s in revolt. If being poor, silenced, a servant, a slave, or a second-class citizen was Women's Business in my culture, then I wanted out. At that point in my life it had become overwhelmingly evident that traditional women's work counted for nothing, and that the dice was loaded against those who crossed the gender boundary to participate fully in decision making at any level of government or industry.

We girls born in the 1940s were collectively responsible for giving birth to the action called the Women's Liberation Movement. At first, being a "Wimmin's Libber" was a hoot. It gave us license to break the rules, those social and cultural protocols designed by men to contain and maintain women within the boundaries of their man-made world. These actions went a long way toward fulfilling my serious hunger to be visible, and eased my anger at being asked to get my little brother to guarantee a motor vehicle loan for me when I had a university education and a secure job as a high school teacher and he had neither. We burned our bras, marched defiantly in trousers instead of skirts, stockings, and high stiletto heels, busted into Men Only bars, stood for university and general elections, and incessantly demanded equality. It was much later that we really understood just how structurally and institutionally disadvantaged women were in Western society. By that time I was married, divorced, and a mother myself, a single parent, the head of my own little family but just as responsible for my child's survival and thriving as all the fathers with whom I competed in the marketplace of paid work, and all the mothers who did volunteer work and homecrafts.

Motherhood came easily and naturally to me and I was not going to let it upset my journey toward equality in my society or culture. My strenuous childhood had equipped me with a fine mind, a sharp tongue, impressive physical prowess, and a finely tuned survival instinct with the competence to carry through whatever I chose to work at. Lingering underneath this persona was a family heritage of generations of teachers, preachers, and missionaries that nudged me toward working in the fields of justice, human equity, and caregiving. My participation in the feminist movement fit this bill but was not enough. Bringing about attitudinal change in adult males never seemed sufficiently satisfying or thorough in its execution. I wanted to *shape* the minds of the next generation of people and mold the next generation of thought. I wanted to see an end to the cultural attitude toward women inherent in the biblical story where Eve is created from Adam's rib for male service and pleasure as though woman were merely an appendage to the male gender. This, I thought, could only be achieved by espousing an equally valid yet uniquely *woman's* way of seeing the host of social, political, and economic issues that the sixties generated. In my private life this meant taking responsibility for my own offspring and as many other disadvantaged children as I could manage. At the age of twenty-four I had my own two-year-old son and three wanton teenage "daughters." By the time I was thirty-four, eleven teenagers of both sexes called me guardian. Even now, years later, I have seven teenage boys and girls in my care or custody in addition to my own teenage daughter.

In everyone's life there seems to be an event or chance encounter that proves to be the inevitable meeting with destiny or fate. For me, this was meeting the charismatic, visionary Ngarinyin Aboriginal Lawman David Mowaljarlai. He emerged as the most profound influence on me until his untimely death in September 1997. Our evolving friendship provided the model, framework, and direction for my thinking, my work, and my ultimate acceptance of my identity as a woman and the role and authority of doing Women's Business.

Gender and Identity Revisioned

In 1973 my son was just three when I was appointed special advisor to the Western Australian Minister for the North West. This job included travel to the remote Pilbara and Kimberley regions of the far north of the state of Western Australia to meet with individuals and groups who had problems or suggestions related to the delivery of government services, and to advise the minister on "quality of life" issues for people living in remote communities.

At that time the Pilbara was a region in transition. There were old mining and port towns whose pattern of settlement had grown slowly over a hundred or so years, following the discovery of gold, stock grazing, shipping patterns, and the availability of water. Then there were new towns, planted in the deserts and on the coast by international corporate giants whose lifeblood was iron ore. The old settlements had character and history; their tiny populations had developed a real sense of community, and lifestyles that reflected and embraced the reality of living in a harsh, hot, geographically isolated area. The new towns were transplanted microcosms of any major city:

artificially stratified to reflect the company hierarchy, fully air-conditioned to simulate a temperate climate, and filled with young families and single men brought in specifically to drive the massive, multimillion-dollar open cut mines.

Aboriginal camps and reserves were found within and around the old communities. Black and white mingled casually and comfortably together while remaining culturally separate and distinct. Whether fossicking for gold, driving cattle, or loading ships, both races were there rubbing shoulders with each other in shared work—not in friendship, but without fear or hostility. Like the heat of the day and the sweat on the brow, they were just there, side by side in a shared reality. The Aboriginal people held to their culture, went Walkabout to perform their ceremony or hunt for bush tucker, and submitted to the sociopolitical doctrine of the day which held they were a class of people believed to be a primitive, less evolved form of human life.

There were no Aboriginal people in the new mining towns. In the early 1970s these towns were closed and access could be gained only with permission and by arrangement with the corporations. They were called company towns. Aboriginal people were not consulted about the mining operations that invaded and excavated their sacred sites and lands. They were simply invisible.

As special advisor, I was to work with Whitefellas only. At first I did not question this. I was a newcomer to the region and had to come to terms with my task, the extreme climate, the experience of driving hundreds of kilometers on bloodred, sandy roads and tracks, and flying in fragile single-engine aircraft that flicked around in the sky on the tropical heat thermals like dry leaves in autumn gusts. I spent much of my time meeting company officials, mischievous unionists, and desperately alienated young mothers.

Until the mining boom of the 1960s and '70s the Kimberley and Pilbara regions were little known. Remote and hostile, majestic and mysterious to the vast majority of Australians who hugged the coast in climatically temperate southern Australia, these regions were dominated by Aboriginal culture and peoples while the European presence was restricted to pioneers, ranchers, eccentrics, and a service population of bureaucrats. In those days Australians knew little of Aboriginal culture, and seemed happy to remain blissfully ignorant. Mining news was the only news that came from the area because mining created jobs and promised wealth to the still youthful state of Western Australia. In the collective consciousness of the cities, this wild country was for men only, a place where they isolated themselves to escape broken relationships or family responsibility, and to earn big dollars. Here they drank hard, swore colorfully, and indulged in that special kind of "blokey" male behavior that seems to emerge when men live without the tempering influence of women, children, and social values.

My headquarters was in the coastal town of Port Hedland, a place divided by a spit of sandy swamp into old Hedland and, twelve kilometers away, the new government settlement of South Hedland. In between them was the Three Mile, an Aboriginal reserve where approximately 150 people lived in unmitigated squalor, invisible to the eyes and minds of the Whitefellas. Each day as I drove from South Hedland to my office, I passed Aborigines walking along the road toward the pub. Like the scrub and marsh, I barely noticed them. It was not until I met a wonderful Aboriginal woman named Rosie that my consciousness awakened to the fact that there was an Aboriginal presence in the region and in all the old towns. She took me to the Three Mile, visited my infant son and I at the hotel, and on weekends, we went bush.

Conferences were very popular in those days. In some respects they were the only opportunity for the people of the north to talk to the remote decision makers who defined, directed, and modified their lives. Sometimes an Aboriginal person was invited to attend a particular session, usually to speak about the Land Rights Movement that emerged in the seventies. I was invariably a speaker at one or another of these conferences, usually in the soft part of the program, where I talked about those quality of life issues that were the domain of women. It was on one of these occasions that I first met Mowaljarlai. During a morning tea break, he stood conspicuously alone by an exit door, ignored by almost all participants, who did not know how to talk to a tribal Aborigine. I was also ignored because quality of life issues were regarded with considerable suspicion. Besides, I was "a bloody feminist." I introduced myself to Mowaljarlai, saying, "We're the odd ones out here!" He laughed and we were instantly united as the odd couple. I was an opinionated twenty-six-year-old feminist, mother of one son, and he was a fiery forty-eight-year-old tribal Lawman, father of eight children. Over the years we sought each other out on these occasions and our friendship grew.

In those heady, revolutionary days, both Mowaljarlai and I saw the world exclusively through the eyes of political activism. Feminism was taking root in both public consciousness and in legislatures around the country. Land Rights was very clearly on the political agenda along with the doctrine of self-management and self-determination. The underlying energy of all these issues was the search for justice. This was often interpreted as equality, which was further interpreted as sameness—all human beings are equal because all are human. It was some years before I acknowledged that we were not, in fact, equal. Neither were we the same. Mowaljarlai and I came from cultures whose underlying myths, philosophies, and ideologies were profoundly different, particularly relating to gender as fact *and* principle.

As a feminist, I had expected and sought equal rights and access to all cultural expressions that were conventionally the domain of males, particularly the political and economic domains. In the context of our personal friendship, the Ngarinyin Lawman Mowaljarlai expected, encouraged, and taught me to restrict myself to and develop skills in Women's Business, while he operated within his cultural paradigm of Men's Business. Split between these two cultural views of gender, I often felt deeply torn. On one hand, I did not intend to surrender any of the hard-fought gains of access and participation in significant decision making. In my day-to-day world, however, a previously denied, deep sense of my own feminine self washed over me. For years I struggled with this conflict and apparent contradiction both in my self-image and in my relationship with the male world.

Because Aboriginal culture was seen as inferior, irrelevant, and even primitive by white Australia, Mowaljarlai was, like Western women, generally diminished, even dismissed as an activist for the unacknowledged underclass. I was a forthright feminist activist, a warrior who fought for women's *and* Aboriginal cultural recognition through the doctrines and law of political and social justice. Because of our friendship, I was able to see my own culture through the perspective of a visionary tribal Lawman of a primary indigenous culture. This unique window on the world opened my eyes to a concept of the feminine whose authority and nature is, I believe, integral to the health and well-being of *all* human societies. Through my friendship with Mowaljarlai I have come to understand the forgotten essence of being a woman in my own culture—which continues to extinguish, or render as invisible as the mother of my childhood, the Essential Feminine.

Mowaljarlai's position as a tribal Lawman for an invisible culture and my position as a female in Western culture were uncannily similar. The relationship between the Western and Aboriginal cultures seemed to be a reflection of the relationship between the feminine and the masculine in Western culture. We enjoyed a mutually enriching discourse on the nature and evolution of gender identity and consciousness that lasted until his death. Using our own decades-long relationship as a base, we created an allegory for a consciously conceived vision and strategy for millennial change.

Mowaljarlai's and my friendship began tentatively, as all relationships do. At first, we sought the familiar to share—family, places visited, issues of mutual interest. We communicated in English because that was the only language I spoke. Mowaljarlai was conversant in five languages, English being the fifth. He had learned to speak, read, and write basic English in the Kunmunya Mission where he spent much of his youth. His command of English was better than that of most tribal Aborigines but was limited to a range of vocabulary and expression given to him by those Whitefellas—religious leaders, anthropologists, lawyers, and government bureaucrats—with whom he came in contact. There were no poets, musicians, artists, metaphysicists, or philosophers among his early European contacts, and few women. In fact, until our friendship, he did not have the vocabulary in English to say what his mind saw and knew, and what he desperately wanted to communicate and share.

It was some years before I understood the intellectual and cultural assumptions, the ideological dogmas that I brought to our friendship. I simply applied them willy-nilly, not thinking that he might conceive and experience the world in a different way. I operated on the assumption that the intellectual tradition to which I was born was the birthright of all humanity, that logic and reason—the myth of logos as I call it now—were not only the default settings of human thought but were absolute values in their own right. I felt I had a kind of intellectual responsibility to encourage Mowaljarlai to see things through my skilled, objective, if passionate, eyes.

As we aged, and our respective families grew and changed, we began to share our children with each other. We were now both single parents, each of us going through our respective passages of life as were our children. The difference between us was that his and his sons' passages were marked by rich ceremony and ritual while mine and my son's passed by uncelebrated. I felt both envious and somehow diminished. His boys were exquisitely aware of their stages of maturation, their identities, and the relationships that bound them in a true sense of cultural and social belonging. My son's and daughter's world was urban, fragmented, and quite detached from any spiritual sense of identity or belonging. Our relatives, all of whom lived thousands of kilometers apart, had little contact with each other. By way of understanding the meaning and significance of the rites of passage that Mowaljarlai and his children celebrated, I asked questions endlessly. It was during these years that I discovered a depth of meaning in the major ceremonial events as well as the most subtle of signals that celebrated these biological changes or emergence of "sight." I also discovered that Men's Business and Women's Business are biologically, not ideologically, grounded, that a division of responsibility by gender liberated both so that they could experience respect for the sovereignty, authority, and potency of each other, that each stage of life carried gender-specific, biologically rooted aptitudes that were evident in social behaviors.

Mowaljarlai's behavior toward me was that of an older Ngarinyin Lawman toward a maturing woman, a mother or Murranburra (an older person with a high degree of cultural knowledge), and a Banman (visionary/healer/teacher). This had both mundane and ideologically heretical implications. At its most mundane, I gradually found myself cooking, cleaning, serving, ironing, and chauffeuring for Mowaljarlai, his fellow Lawmen, and their children. To the great mirth, even shock, of my feminist friends, I waited on the old man hand and foot while he was guest in my home. For my Gardia, or Whitefella, friends and colleagues and my own children it was still "You know where everything is. Help yourself and clean up afterwards!"

Our friendship had a profound impact on my self-concept as a female, challenging my ideologically sound, politically correct beliefs and behaviors. I found that in Mowaljarlai's company I felt so fully alive and potentialized as a woman that I started to reevaluate the doctrine of feminism, particularly what I saw as its choice of a competitive, more masculine personhood over womanhood. I liked the sense of female empowerment he gave me. Mowaljarlai respected what he believed was my authority as a mature woman. When I spoke about the internal workings or processes of anything at all, he listened mindfully and respectfully. I learned that women's authority was integral to the process of all conceptual development because it was my biological birthright as a gestator of life. Motherhood endowed me with that authority. I served him domestically because nourishment, health, and well-being were Women's Business.

It is also Women's Business to perpetuate language in the world as mothers of small children, as the navigators and teachers of adolescents, as wives and grandmothers with their families as they share the joys, tears, and texture of life, as I did with Mowaljarlai in building a bridge of understanding between our two ways of seeing.

One never really knows exactly when or how transformation happens but it happened in our friendship and this was reflected in the pathway we followed from 1989 until his death in 1997. Certainly there were outside events that pushed us to increasingly creative solutions to issues that would neither go away nor be resolved. The Ngarinyin struggle for recognition of their preexisting Native Title was one such issue. Another was our simultaneous recognition that the younger generations were in deep trouble. Their lack of identity as male or female and their lack of direction seemed to be related to the fragmentation and breakdown of cultural and social values, the disappearance of authority structures such as tribes and families, and the ideologically driven extinguishment of gender difference. These generations seemed aimless, rootless, unfulfilled. In their search for meaning, for relevance within society as a whole, they were finding ideologies and institutions that not only failed to inspire or sustain them but that attempted to incarcerate them within the man-made boundaries of a myth they did not relate to.

As we cast our vision wider, we recognized that the biologically rooted social orders of his culture, and the self-correcting and self-managing communities of mine, were all but destroyed. Parental authority had gradually been eroded by the state, and older generations had been rendered redundant, usurped by legislation that created and maintained a level playing field free of age or gender considerations. State social and welfare policy and programs were growing to meet the terrible social consequences of cultural destruction symbolized by the demise of the living myths by which human cultures thrive. We found teenagers being taught *how* to use drugs of addiction recreationally because "drugs are out there, they're a fact of life, and prohibition doesn't work." We found young girls, only just menstruating, being given advice about, and access to, oral contraception and abortion by the state because "nobody wants unwanted pregnancy and nobody can stop kids from having sex when they want to." Sexual depravity and abuse, whose victims included prepubescent boys, girls, and old women, increased daily. Unemployment among young people was running at three times the rate for thirty-year-olds while among Aboriginal people it was nudging 90 percent! More jails were being constructed to incarcerate more male youths. Primary school children bashed up their teachers and burned down schools. Middle-aged mothers were now too frightened to teach their daughters about womanhood, and fathers had become afraid of the political power and potential violence of their sons. Christian churches were either emptying or closing altogether while fundamentalism of all kinds was erupting with a vengeance. Everywhere, everywhere lay the evidence of the decaying human condition because the living myths that inspire the soul had been replaced by the exploitative, man-made myth of economic rationalism. This state of affairs continued to worsen.

Mowaljarlai and I, like parents worldwide, became aware that we could do little to change entrenched institutional ideologies and the policies that were shaping the minds of our children. However, we could direct our energies to raising public awareness about the nature of Men's Business, Women's Business, and rites of passage, and we could still apply this knowledge within and between our families and tribes. It was around this time that the memory of my father's mind-bending exercises in my childhood reemerged with some force. I wanted to find imagery and knowledge that were familiar to people within my own culture in order to relate and amplify the wisdom of Ngarinyin Law. I thought, if their Law relating to Men's Business, Women's Business is biologically rooted, and their claim that the basic unit of existence is that there are always two—male and female, masculine and feminine—there must be evidence of this in the world of science. This search took me into quantum physics where I found absolute consistency between quantum theory and Ngarinyin Law. In the field of genetics, where the basics of DNA is the *relationship* between two chemically encoded strands of life, the story was the same. When I looked into the world of the computer chip, I found that the totality of cyberspace is composed of an infinite range of coded relationships using the digits zero and one. These symbols could just as easily have been a star and a square. Perhaps coincidentally, perhaps insightfully, the Ngarinyin symbol for female is an open circle, and for male, a single stroke. These represent the shape of the womb and the shape of the phallus. In the language of Ngarinyin rock art these two symbols are juxtaposed in an infinite variety of relationships to create pictures and stories, from which Men's Business and Women's Business are derived.

Not only did my intellectual quest look at the scientific for comparisons to Ngarinyin Law, it went the other way as well. In a number of scientific fields I have been able to give a fresh view to problems being addressed by postgraduate students, researchers, and professors by explaining the workings of Ngarinyin philosophy within the relationship of Men's Business, Women's Business. My work has now expanded into the corporate sector where many large organizations, having realized the inefficiency of top-heavy management, a chain of command, and little or no internalized sense of identity or accountability within the lower ranks, are now undergoing radical restructuring. How surprised they are to discover that the ancient Law of the Ngarinyin embodies a relevant, inspiring, organic, sustainable, and dynamic system of management and decision making based on age and gender relationships that profoundly improves productivity and accountability within the modern corporation! It has given me considerable pleasure to return to those very same male-dominated industries and agencies who shunned Mowaljarlai and me as activists in the 1970s to help them find ways of coming to terms with quality of life issues within their organizations.

In the lives of our families, we started teaching the fundamentals of this ancient system of relationship, of Men's Business, Women's Business, through example and directive. Mowaljarlai instructed his sons to observe gender and kinship constraints with my daughter. My son, now twenty-eight years old and a father himself, is navigator and brother to Mowaljarlai's sons. Until Mowaljarlai's death, we taught the Ngarinyin principles in seminars, workshops, and our children's schools. I continue to embody them in my public life of speaking, teaching, and writing, and in my role as mother to Mowaljarlai's sons and caregiver to his grandchildren and other Ngarinyin young people. The sense of identity and belonging we all enjoy, the ease with which our intergenerational relationships are conducted, and the purpose that we inject into our tasks and lives reflect the profound wisdom of the Ngarinyin Law of Relationship.

Where do we go from here?

Men's Business, Women's Business is about more than gender-specific definition and function. That males are physiologically different from females is a generally accepted truism in both cultures even if it is politically incorrect to draw attention to or act on this knowledge in Western culture. In Ngarinyin culture, it is an accepted truism that the physiological process of aging is a destiny that all humans share. For Ngarinyin men and women, it is a given that a male's awareness and behavior will respond to and reflect his stage of biological maturation while a female's awareness and behavior will do the same in accordance with her biological stage of maturity. For women and men, each of these stages is marked by ritual and ceremony, celebrated in sacred song, and respected in life. The Ngarinyin Law for relationship between genders and their distinctive stages of maturation is as complex and coherent as the spiraling DNA molecule whose strands of genes interact with each other according to a predetermined biological blueprint and time clock, derived from previous generations, and spanning life from conception to death and beyond. This is the simplicity and ultimate beauty of Men's Business, Women's Business.

Mowaljarlai and I decided to publish a book that contained this Ngarinyin knowledge. The Ngarinyin method of education is to simply tell a story and let its imagery, atmosphere, texture, and meaning work themselves out in the subconscious part of the mind. By contrast, the Western method is to take a story and intellectualize it, to analyze it for meaning and significance, to spell out all its nuances and subtlety, to summarize it in "how to" steps, then to write about it or put a formulated strategy into practice. We did not want to do that. We believed the power of allegory would do an infinitely better job of identifying the relevance of stories than we could. So we opted to use the Ngarinyin storytelling method to share their knowledge, rather than the Western method of academic discourse. In Part 1 I have created verbal illustrations of precontact Ngarinyin life to tell the story of Men's Business, Women's Business in the ages and stages of maturation, using the language of the imaginal and the poetic, and the imagery of the Mythic. In Part 2 I have applied the same styles; however, many of the stories come from real life, as examples of Two-Way Thinking and Converging Pathways. Key Ngarinyin concepts have been explained only where they have been too difficult to reveal in the stories. The commentaries on Western cultural experiences serve as pointers rather than claiming to be academic analyses or full descriptions. Every individual, family, group, community, corporation, or nation can read this book and find its own relevance.

Men's Business, Women's Business could, in some ways, be the basis of a creed for the next millennium because it offers ordinary people ideas for the conduct of their ordinary lives. The ideas and stories can be applied to real-life situations by anyone who sees fit to do so. *Men's Business, Women's Business* empowers people to take responsibility for their own lives and the future by being mindful and conscientious about living in the present. There is no movement, club, party, or any other organization to join, there is no oath to take, and there is no definitive pathway to walk. This book is about being consciously aware of the cultural processes and institutions that affect men's and women's authority, sovereignty, and the fulfillment of their biological birthright. It is a deeply inward journey that speaks to the soul, often bypassing intellect and reason. It is a journey into the mythic part of ourselves. If collectively traveled, this journey could change the direction and experience of modern culture.

Jutta Malnic

Ngarinyin child from Gibb River station who came to Marunbabidi for Bush University djumba, *or dance.*

Chapter One

Introduction to
the Ngarinyin

An amateur archeologist had been taking photographs of Ngarinyin rock art without permission from the tribal Lawmen of the country. He then prepared a theory of a "mystery race" who came from Asia to occupy the lands of the northern coastline of Australia. He had speculative evidence of this migration and had not spoken to any Ngarinyin about it. They found out about his ideas when he published his theory.

"If he talked to us we would have told him," Mowaljarlai said. "We would have told him we were formed from the Earth. Lai Lai we call it—Creation time when all the world was mud. Wandjina moved in Creation and gave us images in the rocks for our Law. You can see all the evidence of our Creation and origins in the images in the Wunggud rock and in the land. They are all there. We don't make paper law. We are not pen people who write theories about our own origins. We know who we are and where we come from. We come from here, not from overseas. Our ancestors are the first people. Wandjina gave us the Law in those images. We can tell you all about those images and the stories in them because they are our relations. We didn't paint those images ourselves; why would we make it up?

Just Anmorrah [Whitefella] scientists make up those migration sto-ries. Why they do that? We don't know."

Ngarinyin Aboriginal people comprise the largest of the three Wandjina tribes of the northwest Kimberley region of Western Australia.

Their country lies north and west of the Gibb River Road, a dirt road running between Derby and Wyndham to service grazing leases. The leases on Ngarinyin traditional homeland include Theda, Doongan (King Edward River), Drysdale, Gibb River, Mt. Elizabeth, Mt. House, and Beverley Springs Stations. The Ngarinyin people claim the head-waters of the Mitchell, King Edward, Moran, Roe, Prince Regent, Sale, and Isdell Rivers and the Walcott Inlet, as their tribal home.

Together with the Wanumbal people of the Mitchell Plateau, and the Worrora people of the coast and islands from Kalumburu in the north to Cone Bay in the south, the Ngarinyin make up the three Wandjina tribes who are interlocked in the Wurnan system of kinship, land, marriage, and law.

These three tribes are unique in Australia. They are the only primary culture in the world who base their spirituality and law on an icon or image that repeats itself throughout the caves of their country. This is the Wandjina.

While they share ceremony, kinship, and philosophy with other northern Australian tribes they are recognized by other Aboriginal peoples as the Wandjina tribes, unique and strong in the Law. All these northern tribes share a belief system based on a philosophy of relationship, that in all of existence there are always two—two moi-eties (groups), two energies, two genders, two dimensions of existence such as above and below, seen and unseen, action and idea, generative and receptive. The dynamic of relationship holds that neither one is viable without the other, that survival and increase are dependent upon their interactivity, like the dual strands of DNA whose chemical bonds govern the growth and life of an organism.

Like indigenous cultures everywhere in the colonized world, Ngarinyin culture suffered from the devastating impact of European cultural invasion and political sovereignty. Continental Australia was conquered by the British, not through heroic battles but by the application of European civilization's overwhelming ignorance about the land and its peoples, nineteenth-century Christian zeal, religious self-righteousness, and a dangerous belief in their racial superiority, all reinforced by gun powder. The peaceable, Earth-honoring Aboriginal tribes, whose battles with each other were always mythic and ritualized, were easy prey for the predatory, militaristic state police of the Crown of England and easily fell to the diseases, gun power, incarceration, and enslavement used by their self-proclaimed masters.

In the name of the Crown, Aboriginal tribal lands were unilaterally usurped by the flag, pens, and guns of British colonialists. Beginning in the late eighteenth century, colonial proclamations were followed by the establishment of colonial outposts and later government depots. Rangers stationed in these depots toured the bush to rid large areas of land of troublesome humanity, making way for unfettered British settlement. The Wandjina tribes were among the last to be cleared out of their tribal lands, their enforced removal continuing to the early twentieth century.

The North Kimberley was divided up among the Presbyterian, Anglican, and Roman Catholic Churches for missionary work which, they said, was to protect and civilize the natives. The Ngarinyin and Worrora were herded or enticed into the remote Presbyterian mission station of Kunmunya where they were controlled by a benevolent and enlightened missionary, the Reverend Love. Wanumbal people and those of adjoining tribes were collected in the authoritarian Benedictine mission of Kalumburu where the Spanish priests and brothers did their best to extinguish all indigenous law, beliefs, and practices.

When the Swan River Colony, nearly two thousand miles to the south, became a political entity in its own right at the turn of the twentieth century, it assumed complete authority over the vast western third of the continent. In 1896 the fledgling state issued stock grazing licenses in the remote Kimberley, calling them pastoral leases after the eastern Australian land tenure title. These leases were meant to encourage the settlement and development of what was hoped were arable lands in order to feed the small but growing population of the south. However, none of these early drafted leases was taken up. The distance from pastoral station to market was so great even the most optimistic livestock movement projections said it would take up to a year to walk stock to population centers. Other means of transport were virtually nonexistent, the country was extremely rugged, and the ancient soils disappointingly impoverished. Added to these adversities were an inhospitable tropical climate, the prevalence of unknown and rapidly communicated diseases, and an ever-present fear of attack by wild natives. With sheep, herd, and grain stock failures in the East Kimberley, it wasn't until the 1930s that pioneers started to enter the northern Kimberley to try their hands at cattle grazing and the majority of pastoral leases were not developed until the late 1960s. To this day, no single pastoral lease in the Wandjina tribal lands has been economically viable and no grain crop has ever been successful.

Between 1950 and 1970 the Ngarinyin and Worrora tribes were relocated by the government four times, each a step further away from their beloved country. While some of the younger people were prepared to try living within Western culture, many older Ngarinyin and Worrora people returned to their Wunggud or origin places immediately. This drift from government settlements back to their homelands has been constant since these tribes were formally recognized by the Australian government as citizens of Australia in 1967 and were legally free to move within the country without official consent. Nowadays most of the Ngarinyin live in six small communities on their sacred land within the boundaries of pastoral leases issued by the Western Australian government to a handful of Western families. All of these leases are subject to Native Title claim, a process still in effect involving legal recognition of their prior ownership of the land.

As in the rest of Aboriginal Australia, the cost of European civilization's destruction of a cultural system that sustained these people for tens of thousands of years is heavy. For Ngarinyin people under the age of sixty, the old ways are gone forever. Their contemporary life is a hybrid of Ngarinyin philosophy and spirituality in their daily lives combined with impoverished marginalization and its associated despair on the fringes of Western society. Alcohol and alienation have ravaged three generations of Ngarinyin people so far and the prognosis is not good for those now approaching adolescence. The Australian community remains as ignorant of the depth and relevance of Aboriginal culture now as it was when the first fleet of convicts from

Britain arrived on the eastern shores of the continent two hundred years ago. With the exception of a few remote, local schools, no indigenous languages are taught in mainstream educational institutions anywhere in Australia and there are no effective curricula to bridge the ignorance chasm. Aboriginal people and culture are either criminally visible or culturally invisible. Their prior claim to the continent is only now reluctantly being acknowledged, but this movement faces immense political pressure from vested interests and power bases who wish to legally quash their rights altogether.

For elderly Ngarinyin, the old ways are the only ones they know. They were enculturated in the original beliefs, systems, and lifestyle and as they grow older and wiser it is these very values they wish to preserve and teach, not only to their own Ngarinyin young but to the Western world. They recognize that Western culture has created many problems for lands, waters, and the atmosphere shared by all of Creation. They believe that, with only a little time left themselves, they should share their knowledge, wisdom, and insight for the benefit of the Earth and the survival of humankind. They believe that the future will only be sustainable if global consciousness shifts to awareness of what they call Two-Way Thinking—the ways of ancient indigenous cultures in sacred relationship with, and underpinning, the modern worldview.

For the Ngarinyin there is no confusion about identity, status, authority, and gender function for all people and all of Creation. Although the old system has been significantly disrupted since families and tribes have been semidomesticated, Westernized, and Christianized, the original system, self-sustaining for tens of thousands of years, continues to resonate its primary truth in the present day.

Their system of cultural organization is essentially organic, biologically based, and integrated with their environment. It is and has always been a reflection of the way nature operates. Their Law reflects the laws of nature. The Ngarinyin worldview is based on the belief that the primary unit of life and existence is relationship. Mowaljarlai would say, "There are always two," holding up the index fingers of his right and left hands. He never held up two fingers from one hand.

In describing relationship with two hands, he acknowledged that each participant or aspect of the relationship comes from a different side, has different functions and strengths, and responds to different brain or mind messages. Just as it is difficult to tie shoelaces with two fingers on one hand, relationship is not two fingers of the same side. Relationship is the complementary and cooperative input of two separate but joined parts—right and left hands working separately but together.

Ngarinyin philosophy and its reflection in the behaviors known as Men's Business, Women's Business is like the relationship between right and left hands. They are both hands, yet they are physically and functionally different. Together in relationship, they create a harmonious interaction while performing a single function. The Ngarinyin Law governing human function is gender based because they know that although every individual has the ability to survive on his or her own, together in relationship they are able to thrive and procreate, a feat as yet unachievable by a single human.

Although their evident gender relationship occurs in the form of male and female human beings, the Ngarinyin recognize and name feminine and masculine energies in the whole of Creation. Spirit children, as yet unconceived, live in the Wunggud waters or special lagoons waiting to be reflected into being by becoming human. Wunggud waters are female because they were created by Snake who coiled herself up to sleep on her long journey through the land. Snake moved under the ground, coming to the surface every now and then. As she came up, the flat land rose up over her back creating what we call hills. She writhed deeply through other landscapes, creating rivers. She is still there because the hills are still there as are the great river systems. When Snake needed a rest she coiled up to sleep. After awakening, she moved on, leaving a hole or indentation in the ground. Wandjina, the rain, thunder, and creator spirit, emptied his rains onto the Earth and filled up the holes left by Snake. When these indentations were filled with the great Wandjina Spirit's seed rains, the holes became Wunggud waterholes, each filled with new life existing in its birth medium, sacred water. The Wunggud waterhole, like the womb, regularly receives this gift from Wandjina of the heavens, thereby assuring the renewal of Creation.

Spirit children also abide in the Milky Way, protected by its male energy. They project their light from the Milky Way to seed the Wunggud waters with their reflection while remaining in the heavens. You can see them there, playing and sparkling at night, both above the Earth and in the waters.

When a man walks by the lagoon at nightfall, a spirit child jumps from the water into his head. He then sends a dream of the spirit child to his wife. The instant she receives the dream by thinking that a spirit child has entered her head, it pops into her womb and starts to grow. She might have a dream of a family, baby, or child to signify that she has received the spirit child.

Within this conception story is the principle of two energies, male and female. The Milky Way is male. The Wunggud waters are inseminated with spirit children. The waters, which are female, conceive and gestate them until they are ready to become physical through a man and woman. The man inseminates the woman by dreaming the spirit child into her head. She receives or conceives the dream and consummates it through sex, and it instantly becomes a physical reality in her womb which then gestates the physical child.

The Wandjina is male energy, which spills the rains into the hole in the ground, which is female. The hole is created by Snake whose movement is female, opening up the Earth ready for receiving the rains. The Earth is female because on the back of Snake she grows fruits, vegetables, and seeds that feed on her life-giving energy. Snake also creates the watercourses for the rains to fill up and nourish life.

The woman knows she is pregnant because the child inside gives her signs. The primary sign is the cessation of menstrual bleeding. Womb blood is necessary to feed the unborn, to give it identity, form, and spiritual connectedness with the physical world it will soon enter. She changes her diet to special foods that nourish and sustain the power of her womb. Menstrual blood is considered very powerful because it is believed to create perfect human beings. It is unique to women, and its power is feared and revered by men.

The man is from a group of families whose energy is from either the masculine side or feminine side of Creation. In Ngarinyin, those groupings are Wodoi and Djingun. Wodoi are hunting and hunted identities while the Djingun are collecting and collected identities. Males and females belong to both but can only become partners with their opposite. At marriage, the woman carries the Law from her side to his. The Law belongs to men to receive and manage but it is carried through her. In the same way, she carries the seed and offspring of the next generation but the child is received and grown in the man's side or family. Like the warp and weft of a tapestry, the masculine warp framework is given life, design, and integrity by the dynamic, moving feminine weft. This way, there is always balance of gender, Law, role, function, and significance in all of life.

When a child is born it is considered perfect in its potential because it is encoded with the totality of natural law from the beginning of time. The child's life is an evolving realization of its full potential. Each stage of maturation is indicated by either a physical change or a ritual—sometimes both—and marks the fulfilling of potential, a realization of more of the child's function and destiny.

The child is suckled and continuously held by women until it can hold its head up on its own. While the child is believed to be perfect, it is not ready to be separated from human contact because it is dependent on mother's milk for survival. Only when it starts to consume foods other than milk can it be separated from human holding. Touch, smell, the rhythm of the heartbeat, and breathing are considered "food" as necessary for survival as mother's milk. Through these functions, the baby is attuned to its own humanity, and the rhythm or resonance of its group and culture. Alienation or separation from these rhythms of life are considered cruel, tantamount to deprivation and starvation of the child's developing spirit. Provision of the child's spiritual food is seen to be as necessary for healthy growth and development as consumable food. If the child is going to grow to its potential, to be attuned to Earth, nature, the family, tribe, and Law, it must be nourished in this rhythmic life in infancy. As the child grows stronger, becoming more active and interested in the world around her or him, the physical holding lessens, but touching continues.

Child rearing is the responsibility of women and is the focus of Women's Business. Each stage of womanhood carries with it particular responsibilities for the growth and development of the very young. This way, not only are the children given everything they need to grow into their perfection but women grow into their own potential by fulfilling these different roles as they mature. The older teach the younger and in teaching they experience the next stage of their own growth.

When the child starts moving around, it is free to explore the world. This stage coincides with the emergence of baby teeth, the sign that the child is now able to recognize the source of what it wants. Teeth are a symbol of personal authority and their emergence means that identity, resourcefulness, power, and strength of character are developing. The child now recognizes voices, smells, and atmospheres and will respond to naming. The only discipline delivered in these early years is related to safety. When a child moves into a potentially dangerous situation it is simply removed. There is no chastisement or punishment and no doctrine or rules about bad behavior or actions. That comes later in its development.

Since Ngarinyin life is based on the principle of attunement with the world, social conditioning involves the identification and maintenance of harmony, balance, and belonging. This training also includes, of necessity, the recognition of discord, danger, and other imbalances in life systems. Socialization of children is dominated by the Law of Relationship and attunement, including relationships with people, animals, nature, the Earth, and the heavens. It also means that the ideas of individuality, ownership, separation, and possessions do not exist because they have no relevance in Ngarinyin life. In fact these values would be destructive because they are the source of competitiveness, alienation, and unbalanced power relationships. In other words, dominion, or dominance by an individual, species, tribe, or culture, is seen to be against natural law.

When the child is mobile, it can walk to what it wants for its survival—food, warmth, shelter, touch, and comfort. From the stage of mobility to the stage of changing teeth, the child learns from and is encouraged to copy older people in the performance of their duties, recreation and leisure, and ceremony. Children are considered full participants in daily life as well as being the focus of attention while they are awake.

Fathers, uncles, and older men have a special role at this time. While younger men and adolescent boys are expected to cooperate with curious children, older men introduce them to the imaginal world of myth through storytelling, dance, song, music, body painting, and ceremony. The creative dreamworld is important for well-being and it is Men's Business to introduce the child to its imaginal and creative potency. This is done through children's participation in some adult ceremony and ritual, humor, telling special stories about children, playacting, and role-playing. By these means children learn the significance of animals, plants, elements like the sun, moon, stars, night and day, and the sacred relationships that their tribe has with them. The child grows with a holistic view of the world, knowing that all existence has rights, obligations, dangers, benefits, and place. Everything in the child's world has its own story, from a small pebble in the sand to bark on a tree to the sound of a bird. By the time the child loses its first tooth, it has learned the basics of ecology, astronomy, and meteorology as well as animal and plant behaviors and their applications through the creative realms of story, dance, and song. Children know much of the kinship or relationship system into which they and their relations—the animals and plants—fit. They know that there is right behavior and wrong behavior throughout the natural world. They therefore have a comprehensive basic knowledge of natural law by the age of approximately seven years.

When the second teeth start to grow, the child's training begins in earnest because children are expected to apply their knowledge to the way they behave. As these teeth take root and grow, their thinking and competency in the application of Law expands. The child is also prepared for the next stage of its maturation—girls to womanhood and boys to manhood. Children also take on some responsibility and begin contributing to the well-being of infants in the tribe. They actively assist in collecting food, water, wood, and medicinal plants, and they undertake some tasks in food preparation. They hunt for goanna, collect yams, berries, fish, turtle, and cherubim (freshwater crustaceans). Older men and women reflect this development and maturation with stories and ceremonies with higher degrees of sophistication. Children are actively encouraged to tell stories, relate their dreams, and take their place in group activities of all kinds. At puberty, life changes dramatically for both boys and girls.

Girls' biology determines that at a certain stage of physical maturation they begin to menstruate. Menstruation starts when a girl's biological clock tells her body to start releasing an egg a month, an event that will occur for the next forty years. The cycle generally goes full circle every twenty-eight days, identical to the waxing and waning of the moon. Only pregnancy, lactation, and severe trauma stop this cycle from turning year in, year out within the woman.

The eggs have been there since before she was born. While in her mother's womb, the eggs absorbed the mother's resonance and attuned themselves to the maternal heritage or memories much the same way all body cells attune themselves to their surrounding cells and body functions. This means that, although she is a newly emerging woman when she starts her bleedings, a girl has already stored the knowledge and experience of her mother while her eggs have both her and her mother's native knowledge. Every female egg therefore contains three generations of experience and destiny while being linked to the moon and its eternal cycle.

When the girl's menstruation starts, her status, role, and function within the group changes. Her first bleed is celebrated by women while she becomes taboo to adolescent boys and men. She will now be prepared for full womanhood, a process of many years during which her nipples change from a pinkish color to a deep burgundy-brown and her skin also darkens; only then is she considered ripened like a berry and ready to conceive a child. Conception is considered unlucky or illfortuned if her body has not fully ripened, and the offspring is likely to be damaged during birth or be a weak, sickly child.

During these years a young woman's learning takes place under the tutelage and navigation of older women—breeding women, Lawwomen, and healing women—who teach her the inside knowledge of Women's Business. This includes: group and individual survival business like food collection, classification, and preparation; habitat maintenance, including cleanliness of the camping area, water sampling and collection, general hygiene, making cooking fires, collecting firewood, and fire technology; shelter construction; weather forecasting; child rearing; and caregiving. Medical arts are demonstrated including medicine preparation from the extensive pharmacopoeia derived from plants and animals. Girls learn the songs, rituals, and dance for ceremony, touch-healing, and clan dietary management. They gain self-knowledge through attunement to body, mind, and spirit including dream memory and meaning, body rhythms, personal dietary needs and cycles, and intuition and visioning, or seeing in women's specific way.

This training and learning is vigorous and constant whether the growing woman is awake or asleep. The trainee gradually learns an automatic empathy with her environment and her place in it. In addition, she becomes sensitized to the immense resource of her own female potency. She learns to read the world through her maturing womanhood, her ripening body, her cyclic womb. In this way, she is able to understand the processes of nature, the cycles of all seeds, roots, placental and metamorphosing animals, their time and space requirements, their behaviors and illnesses. She becomes attuned to the rhythms and cycles of the entire natural world and natural order.

Only then is she ready to bring her own seed, her own offspring, into the world.

For boys, the process is the male way. As a boy's maturation progresses, his body starts to masculinize, signified by the appearance of pubic hair, the strengthening of his musculature, and the occurrence of wet dreams or night emissions. As these changes happen, both men and women are aware that it is time for him to move out of the world of women into the realm of his destiny, into the fathers' world and his manhood. The crossing over from childhood to manhood is different for him simply because a girl does not leave the world of the mothers whereas a boy must leave to fulfill his maleness, his masculine potency. A girl spends her whole life connected intergenerationally and biologically to her gender world whereas the boy's journey in maturation is in steps and stages of separation. The first separation happens in utero when he breaks from the femaleness of a very young fetus and becomes male inside the female. At birth he is severed from his mother, his placenta is buried in the Earth, and his umbilical cord is hung around his mother's neck until it has dried completely. Then he is eased from his mother's milk to become physically independent of her while continuing to be tied emotionally and spiritually. At puberty, this dependence must be severed cleanly and clearly and ritualized emphatically so the boy is scarred for life by his passage from the childhood world of mothers to the manhood world of fathers.

In a dramatic enactment of severance, the boy is carried away from the world of mothers and is taken to a Men's Business ceremony area where, amidst powerful ritual dance, he is prepared for the start of his manhood journey. The culmination of this ceremony is a symbolic severance from the world of mothers by circumcision. The boy's foreskin is cut and buried in the Earth, uniting his totemic spirit with the Earth Mother instead of the biological mother. When the wounding is completed, he begins his journey into manhood under the tutelage of older men other than his father.

The young man's world is dominated by his biological reality, the emergence of intense sexual drive, and the masculinization of his entire body, mind, and spirit. He must now learn to protect, defend, and *enable* the Motherworld to maintain the tribe through their Women's Business. It is this world womb that will receive his own seed when he has fully matured so it is in the best interests of himself and the group that he conduct himself with discipline and vigor. To achieve this, he learns that he must grow and develop into the male power that has been liberated in his body.

To be able to protect and defend the Motherworld, a youth must learn the complex Wurnan, the land-kinship pattern and texture in which Women's Business operates. Since the Motherworld is generally focused around waterhole habitats, he learns about the natural laws of watercourses, hills and mountains, plains, deserts, vegetation patterns, and animal movements and habitats—in other words, the macroworld and its workings.

He is guided to this knowledge by older men who take him to visit camps, kin, and tribes. He learns their languages, customs, and diplomatic or ceremonial obligations. In distant yet specific kinship or Wurnan groupings he will find his wives. En route he is taught hunting, tool and weapon manufacturing, paint-clay sites and their ceremony, and the song cycles for all his tribal and tribally connected lands. There are dangers, even death, to challange him on his journey but he must face and transcend these. This is how he learns survival, obedience, endurance, and self-discipline. By meeting these challenges, his own drive for action is satisfied.

Men's Business includes all the natural law systems in which the tribe survives and thrives. It includes navigation by the stars, recognition of time and place relationships based on the moon, climate, and weather patterns, and myth and ceremony communicated by the ancestral beings who created and "gifted" the land to the tribes. Men's Business also covers the expressive arts and skills of song, dance, and painting, each of which requires its own specific rituals, sequences, and observances, as well as knowledge of the consequences of getting them wrong or failing to meet the obligations. The Law is vast, complex, and subtle, and a maturing male must learn all of its detail and nuance. This requires extraordinary self-development and knowledge of the self-correcting powers inherent in the natural order. He learns how the natural world signals events, dangers, accidents, truth, lies, and destiny. His many tests and challenges must be met courageously yet fearfully, with correct attitude and centered spirit. Punishments are delivered without fear or favor because they are themselves projections of the natural law. A man may be speared in one leg or both legs for a serious offense, sent away from his clan, or "sung." When a man or woman is sung, the curse or punishment is directed at his or her spirit. Lawmen chant their intent of sickness or death to the offender, who may be hundreds of miles away. The offender's spirit is always affected. No punishment is negotiable. If a punishment does not take place, the Earth or the cosmic energies will retaliate with a major self-correction.

Ceremonial ritual and dance play a significant part in Men's Business and an initiate must be in command of the basics. These ceremonies relate to other ceremonies being performed by other tribes and groups along Song Lines—energy meridians in the land—so that full song cycles are completed. The song cycle, or singing up the country, reflects the stars, winds, smells, temperatures, and visual land forms by which travelers navigate. The country will reveal itself only if the song cycle is performed correctly and the dance rhythm emits and evokes the right vibrations. Song and dance are not separate art forms. They are the means by which humans interact with and attune to the resonances of Earth, the heavens, and all plants, animals, and land forms. It is only through the constant maintenance of these unseen networks of Earth magnetism, cosmic winds, energies, and the communication waves of universal existence that the health and well-being of the tribes in their lands can be guaranteed. This is the Men's Business that the initiate must learn.

As he matures and grows bigger, stronger, and leaner, he learns more of the depth, sophistication, and complexity of the human Law that reflects the laws of nature, its maintenance and management. He learns that relationship is the Wurnan, the system that weaves every expression of existence in the tapestry of Creation. All of this law business finds expression and life in hundreds of stories. The only way humans can comprehend the immensity of the natural world is through the imaginal world, the mythic form where philosophy and law find their full expression. Men's Business is responsible for the maintenance of the mythic which ensures that the group, environment, and culture thrive.

When the youth starts to grow hair on his forearms and his whiskers change from soft down to bristles, he is considered ready for marriage and the procreation of the next generation. He has learned all of the basic laws of keeping harmony and balance in the world, how to physically survive in all situations, how to hunt and take up his general responsibilities with the other men in the tribe, to protect the Motherworld, and to respect and honor Women's Business and the universal feminine.

The rites of passage from childhood to adulthood, which culminate in marriage and procreation, are the most significant in Ngarinyin life. They mark the eternal cycle of birth, transformation, and regeneration, the pathway of life to death and rebirth.

The Ngarinyin world is one of a never ending present that turns in its own natural cycle through all phases of becoming. It is a literal, visceral world where time, space, and measurement exist only in the context of the moment. Unfettered by intellectual constructs which, by definition, restrict the validity of experience to the ability of language to describe it, the Ngarinyin receive the world in its totality and enact it in their mythic life. Their humanity is expressed as a reflection of the natural world and natural order. They are unencumbered by the worldview that intellectually rationalizes experience to suit the perpetuation of any power whose primary function is to whip the natural order into submission under the control of its human masters.

While the Ngarinyin of today continue to be psychologically and spiritually dominated by the perspectives, beliefs, and teachings of their original Law, Western colonization has resulted in their inability to sustain the old lifestyle. As in most places where traditional Aboriginal peoples survive, the majority of Ngarinyin people under the age of fifty have been born and raised in special settlements provided by the government. In these settings the old ways have no grounding other than in the memories of the elderly. Neither do tribal Law and lifestyle generate those Western skills necessary for successful settlement living. As a consequence the current generations are captives of two cultures, neither of which they are able to participate in fully. Their reality is alienation from the land on which their Law is based, and marginalization from Western society, in which they must find relevance for their future.

Unfortunately time is running out for the old Law and its adherents. The elder men and women of the original culture are spending their last years putting into place their vision for the future. Through a range of private Western institutional mechanisms focusing on education, the arts, publications, and media, the Ngarinyin, in collaboration with a dedicated network of Whitefellas, are creating the framework for a respectful, dynamic, cocultural future.

Jutta Malnic

Wunggud water following Snake's trail in the land. Photo taken at the crossing on the track to Marunbabidi.

Chapter Two

The Seed

Conception and Birth

It was coming into the Big Wet, the annual monsoon season of tropical Australia. I was noticeably pregnant with my second child, and traveling to visit friends and colleagues in the Wessel Islands of northeast Arnhem Land in the Arafura Sea. I had not been there for more than six months and was welcomed joyfully. The old men, Lawmen of Elcho Island, viewed me with mirth, speaking animatedly to each other in their own language while casting mischievous glances my way. One old man finally said in English, "You bin dreaming lately?" at which point the rest broke into guffaws of laughter, slapping their sides. "Might be somebody else bin dreaming too, eh?" he continued, again accompanied by raucous mirth. I lowered my eyes, feigning embarrassment, yet smiling at their pointed remarks. "You seen any helicopter pilots 'round here?" I asked. "Whitefella one—really good, strong one!" They burst into laughter again then led me away for private discussions. They were being very cheeky, drawing attention to my condition and seeking information about the father. Yet they were acknowledging my pregnant state in the context of their own conception beliefs as a mark of respect.

It is late afternoon. Daughter Sun is bleeding slowly, painfully at the end of her journey, having been bitten by Snake at noon. She is about to reach the fork of the tree where she will hang, oozing blood into the horizon until she drops, too weak to continue feeding Earth with her nourishing light and warmth.

Hunters are returning to their camp. They walk rhythmically along the creek bank, taking in the changes reflected in the water. Sometimes clumps of lily pads hide the world reflected into being. A waterhole, sacred Wunggud waters reflecting the world's transition from day to night, shimmers with the image of the hanging Daughter Sun, urging the hunters homeward with her dying light. This Wunggud, like so many others, contains Creation's ancestral spirits awaiting their transformation into physical being in their continuous dance of renewal. Seething with life and energy, the sacred waterhole releases a spirit child to the newly married hunter as he follows the others on the trek homeward. He experiences an inner pulse, glances at the waterhole, notes the darkening images swirling within, and walks on.

He is quiet that evening, retiring early to his camp with his wife. He notices the particularly bright Milky Way, his ancestors blinking so clear and powerful, enveloping the world in their guiding brilliance, and he feels secure in the knowledge that he and his tribe are protected. As he drifts into that altered state between awake and asleep an image appears in his vision. Like a dream but not the dreaming of sleep, the image becomes a small baby boy lying in his mother's arms, gurgling his infant laughter as he reaches his tiny hands upward, trying to catch the warm wind that blows across his face. The young man jolts with recognition. Smiling, he falls into deep sleep.

The women too have been hunting and gathering this day, as they do most days. Near the waterhole where they camp are dense grasses, bushes with berries for eating and grinding, roots for healing. Goanna, grubs, fruits, and yams are in abundance at this time of year, and the waterhole yields lily roots, fish, turtles, and worms for the taking. With the children running around, exploring, imitating the aunts and mothers, the women pick, pluck, and trap all that they can carry, all the while explaining the world to the children, telling stories that name their relationships to everything they encounter. They stop to make a little cooking campfire for the goanna and bread which they eat and feed to the children. The women rest, sort foodstuffs, peel and prepare food for the evening, and talk. Then kicking the coals under to extinguish all danger of fire, they pack up their baskets and bags and turn for home. As they near the camp, they collect firewood and carry it on their shoulders. By the time the hunters return, the fires are lit, water is collected and boiling, and the smell of fresh, cooked bush tucker soon wafts into the surrounding landscape.

Laughter, stories, and joking accompany eating around the camp-fire. There are stories of episodes on the hunt. One about somebody's misadventure, his name veiled, is stretched out for all its nuances. It brings guffaws and shrieks from the men and women. Children play-fight with sticks, and wander in and out of conversations, completely secure in their place in the extended families. They are gently chastised for mischief but not punished. After the stories the new wife joins her husband at their camp.

Her sleep is fitful. She is niggled by a vision that forces itself into her dreaming, a powerful image of small children playing slippery-dips down a muddy bank into a safe part of the lagoon. No saltwater crocodiles can enter this place, only "freshies"—smaller, narrow-nosed freshwater crocs which do not attack humans. One of the little boys looks at the wife with a glimpse of recognition yet she hasn't seen him before. She watches the children, watches him. Again he looks at her knowingly, somehow claiming her. The vision dissolves while the memory of that particular boy lingers, intensifying in her mind. Her body jolts. The spirit child has been planted.

She mentions the dreamlike vision to her husband and perhaps to her aunties. Her husband confirms that he also had a dream in which a spirit baby visited him. Later this recollection will verify the conception time, the child's paternity, and the Wunggud place from which their child derives his Gi spirit. It is full moon time and the nights are bright with its soft candlelight shining against the backdrop of the radiant starlit void. Bright Moon, whose inhabitants—the brother and his female dog, spun out to space in Creation time—are now clearly visible. She notes this particular moon for no particular reason except that its shine seems to carry special energy for her. And she did have that vision. Full moon time is usually filled with light, bright happiness within the camp, a reflection of its radiant cycle.

As the moon starts his waning the tribe continues its daily ritual of food hunting and gathering, tool manufacture, medicine preparation, water collecting, shelter maintenance, storytelling, and ceremony. Every evening there is dancing and singing just for pleasure and to confirm the tribe's place in their country.

One day, two moons later, the hunters bring back a big emu. This is prepared for cooking and eating, a feast of succulent white steaks. The flesh of the emu, usually delicious, tastes uncharacteristically watery. Everyone gasps, immediately realizing it must be a Wunggud spirit Emu. They speculate on its meaning, knowing it to be a significant sign, guessing that someone in their group is with child, thinking it is probably their recently married kinsfolk. The young woman knows it must be a sign for her. It is the totemic spirit of the child she now knows she is carrying. Her husband knows it too but neither speak of it with certainty to each other or to anybody else. But they know. They all know. It is indelibly written in the minds of all who prepared to share this Wunggud Emu.

As her pregnancy becomes evident it is shared quietly, almost secretly, with other women. This is Women's Business so it is considered indiscreet, even rude, for it to be referred to directly or discussed by men. They simply go about their business and prepare the father for parenthood and full status within the tribe. Older women extract oils to rub on the pregnant woman's belly. They protect her, teach her what to eat, what to avoid, and prepare her for the birth of her child. She must not eat bandicoot with claws, nor goanna or turtle because these might make the baby "slow." When her time comes, the women take her to their special place for birthing, dig a pit in the ground and place rocks on either side of it so that the woman can kneel comfortably on the rocks. They prepare a fire, collect water, special leaves and herbs, and sing. Far away in another camp, the men and adolescent girls with their old women guardians watch the children. The father is taken to a special place some distance away where older men loosen all his restrictive clothing and tie a hair belt around his girth. He holds the ends of the belt in his hands and tightens it to support himself. He lies back with his legs wide open and pulls on the belt ends to assist his wife to give birth to their child with his energy. He opens himself up to breathe in the wind, creating an open channel through his body. His breathing simulates the breath of labor, the breathing, birthing Earth. He transmits his energy and breath to his wife.

The women attend the birth, assisting its process with song, rubbing, chanting, warmth, medicines, and reassurance. As soon as the baby emerges he is held by one of the women while the mother births the placenta. Women take the placenta and prepare for its burial, singing the song of completion, returning to the Earth that was born of the Earth, a celebration and acknowledgment of life's cycle of birth, death, and renewal. The umbilical cord, already detached from the mother, is not finally tied off for another week, after which it is hung around the mother's neck where it stays until the baby can crawl. At birth, the child is named after his father's skin group, ancestors, and country, his mother's country, and his birthplace. Then he is taken back to the camp to be offered to the father and all of the kin. The father is ritually consecrated in the completion of manhood, assuming greater responsibility and stature within the tribe. A celebratory djumba, or song and dance ceremony, is then performed by all the kinsfolk, giving the newborn his song for life.

There is great rejoicing at the birth of a healthy child. The little baby is checked all over his body for a sign of his Gi, the totemic spirit of the animal or plant whose spirit entered him, giving him a special relationship with the natural world. The mark is found—a small indentation on the ribs which denotes Emu. When the baby is a couple of months old, he is also named after his totem in a smoking ceremony according to the sign that appeared months earlier when the big emu tasted watery after cooking. In this ritual, rocks are heated in a campfire and placed in a specially prepared pit. Particular leaves from local trees and algae from the Wunggud waterhole from which the baby's spirit came are placed on the rocks to create aromatic smoke. The baby is held over this, turned and rolled so that the smoke suffuses him with the spirit of his totem and country. His kinsmen, painted in the ochres and symbols of their own Gi totems, name him in song and chant, stamping him with his Emu identity. It's a confirmation that the spirit of the Wunggud Emu entered this unborn child, claiming him with its energy. He must serve the emu for the rest of his life. He must refrain from eating its flesh and diligently protect it from harm and abuse. In this way, he will constantly recollect his embodiment and reflection of this expression of Wunggud. He is joined with nature through this ceremony and woven into Wurnan, the pattern of life within his birth country, its ancestral history and experience, and the heritage of country from his mother's side and father's side.

Daughters are equally treasured and until puberty treated the same. From birth, a daughter is promised to her future husband who, if an adult, has special responsibilities to the girl's mother and father, and immediately assumes his role as a named provider for his future wife's family.

The pattern of kinship, of relationship, among all people is a delicate web of interwoven humanity. As each newborn is named into this pattern, Wurnan is strengthened and renewed in a reflection of the great pattern of life.

The newborn is constantly held in someone's arms or in a body-hugging pouch. A small tassel made from the soft tail of a young possum is tied around his tiny wrist, a sensory plaything to stimulate his skin and vision. Because the baby has several mothers and many other attendant family members, he is in constant touch with the human vibrations of heartbeat and breathing. He experiences continuous stimulation and care provided by a procession of kin who respond to his every need, including suckling. The baby is never separated from people or the Earth. He grows with wind in his hair. Not until the baby gets his first tooth and begins to move out of the receptive, immobile stage of development does he touch the ground, or leave the pouch or arms of caregivers.

For the next several months the world is introduced to the child. Mothers and aunts tend his every need as kin absorb him into their consciousness. The Wurnan is gently rewoven to embrace him, to envelop his past, present, and future, guaranteeing his place in the pattern for all eternity. He is named according to his relationship with every man, woman, and child. He is named by his totem. He is named according to his moiety, Wodoi or Djingun. Before he can crawl or walk he has been named by every relationship in the extensive Wurnan kinship system, and in nature.

According to the old beliefs, naming is claiming. The act of naming is ritualized in every new exposure and experience. Naming invokes the subtle energies of Creation to root the newborn's place within it. The child's identity is formed and consolidated in this process, because it defines all his relationships, and therefore the rights and obligations inherent in them. His name is a reflection of all relationships that define his being in his past, present, and future. It claims him as having primary responsibility for guaranteeing constant respect for and maintenance of all relationships in which he is named.

Wunggud is the source and energy of Creation. It is also the *intent* of Creation. Wunggud is both the dynamic *and* fabric of dreaming, that nonphysical reality that is the relationship between the unseeable void and the physical world. Everything that exists is a reflection of Wunggud. Water is the medium through which Wunggud changes from idea to form. Wurnan is the physical expression of Wunggud. The pattern or blueprint of energy relationships that constitutes Wunggud is reflected in Wurnan.

The conception of a child begins in the waters where Wunggud power is concentrated. These waters are the embodiment of sacred relationship, where above meets below, where being mingles with nonbeing. This is analogous to the idea of the structure of an atom changing its form from one entity to another through the notional dynamic of the quantum leap. Dreaming gives ideas shape and form or fabric. In observing the Wunggud, the young husband interacts with the spirit child from the Wunggud and then transmits this to his wife in the fabric of dreaming. She receives the spirit child in dreaming form. The interaction of conscious awareness in both parties brings the idea into physical reality and conception happens. There can be no conception without dreaming. Otherwise women would be constantly pregnant and they are not. The child is named through this process that acknowledges the fabric of dreaming as the source of the child and Wunggud power.

Ancestral energy exists in the Milky Way and is reflected in the Wunggud water which is empowered by the Earth's subtle energies as Wunggud power. This power is projected to a prospective father in the fabric of a spirit child through dreaming. Birth and death are therefore events in a continual cycle of rebirth and renewal. Ancestors include human, animal, and mythic characters that exist simultaneously in all dimensions in an everlasting present. Every newborn child derives ancestral memory and insight by this means.

At birth, the placenta, which nourishes the unborn, is returned to the intimate, infinite womb of the Earth. This rite recognizes the Earth's constantly pregnant state by offering the placenta to nourish brothers and sisters, be they insects, plants, or animals. All of these beings are recognized as kin and belong in Wurnan along with the newborn.

Gestation and midwifery is Women's Business. Childbirth, however, is the product of the relationship between man and woman. A father assists in the process of childbirth by encircling himself in a hair belt made by the mother and her women kin, binding himself to her through the energies residual in her hair. He shares her suffering and assists her by spreading himself in such a pose as to maximize the flow of the breath of life inherent in the wind. He is attuned to the mother energetically, notwithstanding separation or distance, recognizing the power and essence of the subtle energy that binds one to the other as their child is birthed. At any time in the birth process, he can tell what is happening to his wife because of his own experience. The hair belt is kept to be used again when a son reaches puberty.

The smoking ceremony consecrates the child into the tribe and tribal consciousness. At no stage is the child given an individual identity that marks him as an ego separate from the context of his birth, kin, surroundings, or tribal lands. In utero, the child is part of a larger pattern, a system of kinship that spans thousands of years within the tribal country. The child's name is derived from the past, the present, and the future, which exist simultaneously. Even though early childhood care is primarily the mother's responsibility, child rearing is a group function. Women are responsible for the daily management of small children and babies. The child grows up unaware of the concept of self and individuation. In an egocentric sense, individuality has no place in tribal life nor in the Wurnan. To give the individual importance would inevitably result in competition of egos. One cannot belong in Wurnan and be egocentric at the same time. From birth, a child's consciousness is made aware of the pattern of life in which she belongs. Everyone introduced to the child must fit him into their own relationship pattern and consciousness and honor him in that place forever. Wurnan is therefore fixed because it is the Law, yet mutable because it undergoes the changes inherent in dynamic Creation. In Wurnan there is a place to belong for everything and everyone.

From birth a Western child is quietly and meticulously enculturated with a sense of self, of individuality. The process begins with her experience of separation. After the child is separated from the womb she is also physically separated from her mother and all other human beings by clothing, a crib, the concept of quiet, and a separate bedroom. She is also separated from the natural world which she will gradually learn to control and dominate. Born in a hospital, transported in vehicles, enclosed in a carriage, she is moved from one internal space to another.

In Western culture a first baby is usually a joyous event, yet too often new motherhood is a lonely, frightening, and wearying experience which is endured silently and courageously. The mother is generally the primary caregiver for the young baby because the father usually has to work full-time. After a week of help from significant other adults, the mother is usually left to fend for herself. It is her responsibility to cater fully to her baby's needs in addition to maintaining the domestic environment as she did prior to the birth. She does this within the confines of her home. Visitors do pop in to see them both but she spends a large part of her time alone with the baby. Separated from neighbors, the community, and the world by physical structures and the demands of new motherhood, a young mother may well feel isolated and become depressed. She frequently does not have an extended family, sisters, a circle of women, or alternative caregivers on tap. These all must be arranged by her to fit in with the busy schedules of others. With sleepless nights, little communication with the world, and total responsibility for the health and well-being of herself and her child, she is often exhausted, stretched beyond endurance.

A fundamental philosophical difference exists between the Ngarinyin Aboriginal worldview and the Western worldview. This is reflected in the attitudes and behaviors surrounding the beginning of new life. For the Ngarinyin, the fundamental basis of all existence is relationship. In Western culture, the basic unit of existence is the individual. Each culture's beliefs and customs are built on these premises. Ngarinyin culture is sociocentric. Primary social consciousness relates to group integrity and cohesion at the expense of individual ego awareness or development. Western culture is egocentric whereby primary social consciousness relates to independent individual development at the expense of group consciousness.

Ngarinyin belief relating to conception and birth confers the greatest of significance on its place in the renewal of life, its testimony to a higher or greater plan, and the spiritual ceremony and ritual that aligns the Law of Wurnan with the law of nature. Celebration centers around the identification of place and belonging in the Wurnan pattern, and commitment by all to naming their relationships to that place. By naming all relationships in this way, the newborn is woven into Wurnan. Once this naming is enacted, the baby's membership in the tribe is confirmed and made sacred, and all tribal members assume responsibility for him or her. This obliges women and men to provide for the child's mother and father, to support them as they integrate the child into tribal life, and to assume responsibility for caregiving as needed. The new mother is rarely alone with her offspring. She has any number of able kin to share the inevitable demands and responsibilities that a newborn generates. Within this group are children, and women of all ages to hold the child, sing to it, tell stories, rock, feed, carry, warm, soothe and comfort, clean and heal.

Western culture's primary social unit is nominally the nuclear family, comprising at least one parent and one child. Within the family, however, the individual rights of each member take precedence over the integrity and cohesion of the family as a whole. Individual rights are enshrined in law, and are protected by the state. As a result, the primary relationship in Western culture is between an individual and the state. This has the effect of subtly absolving all other adults from responsibility for the child.

Conception is simply the fact of fertilization resulting from the act of sexual intercourse between a man and a woman. The manner in which gestation and birth are managed is usually the individual choice of the mother. Naming a child is an absolute parental choice with no requirement to identify heritage, ancestry, or any spiritual dimension.

Western mothers are seen as the primary caregivers for all the child's needs. No relations, neighbors, or community are obliged to assist or support in any way, though they often do. Government health care agencies, clinics, and independent special interest support groups exist for the benefit of mothers and children but at night these service personnel are usually at home in their own worlds, their responsibilities to their clients finished for the day. Spiritual or religious consecration is less and less frequently an integral part of the celebration or acknowledgment of new life, and neither church congregations nor the religious communities have any official obligation to mother or child.

Within the boundaries of the state's protective laws, however, Western mothers enjoy the freedom of choice. In the absence of prescribed religious and institutional protocols and obligatory customs parents are able to make decisions based on their own research, thought, discussion, and intuition.

One of the most enjoyable aspects of pregnancy and childbirth is the availability of information and its exploration and discussion. It is an intellectually and emotionally active time which is usually savored at many levels. The fact of choice adds the excitement of responsibility to the whole experience and challenges mothers in particular to be informed about the whole process.

Freedom of choice and the rights of an individual are the most cherished values of Western culture. No Ngarinyin has that freedom or those rights. Their world is largely predetermined, their destiny of relationship prescribed in the Wurnan Law of marriage. They are always safe in the knowledge that in the Wurnan relationship system, no one can be conceived alone, be born alone, grow alone, or die alone. Individuality and choice simply do not exist. Today this system is in grave peril. Western influence and law have undermined sociocentricity, tribal living, and the Wurnan system, all of which are written in land they no longer own, and from which most have been removed. Their beliefs remain largely intact but are now memories of the past, no longer grounded in the lands that gave them life and relevance. Their rich practices are rapidly disappearing.

Yet for Westerners there is much to learn from the Ngarinyin. Many Western women are attracted to the ideas of home birth, shared women's responsibilities, collective childrearing, naming ceremonies, and more. Many men are impressed by the significance of ancestral naming, a separate male role in childbirth, and active involvement in specific childrearing responsibilities. Both men and women are attracted to the concept of deep involvement and sharing with extended family and community. Particularly attractive is the higher value ascribed to a social group and its autonomy than to the individual and his or her rights. Perhaps the loss of relevance and meaning inherent in primary social units as a result of freedom and choice of the individual has been to Western culture's detriment. Perhaps conception, gestation, and childbirth are celebrations of the continuity of life for everyone to actively share and enjoy rather than an individual's crowning achievement.

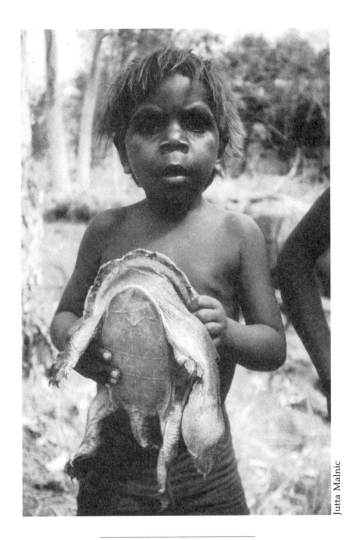

Jutta Malnic

A young Gideon Mowaljarlai holding a freshwater turtle, caught during a camping trip with his father and brother.

Chapter Three

Wuudu Time

Early Childhood

On a typically hot, dusty December day, we met under the bough shelter at Mowanjum, an Aboriginal community in the West Kimberley of Western Australia. The old Lawmen and I had been talking about politics and land, wondering if Australia would ever recognize preexisting Native Title. Young children played around under the water tap in the sand. I brought out a cooler of water, a packet of biscuits, and a bag of oranges, and offered them all around. The remainder sat on the table. A young boy of about seven climbed up onto the table and took an orange. Immediately one of the old men, soon joined by the rest, exclaimed emphatically to the young lad, "Arrh! You can't do that! You can't take that orange! You have to ask. She our mother!" Gently chastised thus, the lad looked at me pleadingly. I nodded okay. He took the orange and ran off. The old men shook their heads, laughing at the innocent ignorance of the little boy. "He gotta learn, that little boy. We don't do that. We don't take that food unless we given it. He have to learn to respect mother. She give us our food. He gotta learn that thing."

It is early morning, before Daughter Sun has begun her journey through the sky. The soft violet and rose hues of daybreak are being raked up by the retreating magenta darkness. Night black, whose weight had pressed down on all the world to induce sleep, slowly lifts to lightness, relieving slumber of its compressed heaviness, freeing living spirits for the pleasure of another day. The land is presunrise sepia, a suggestion of itself. Silhouettes take form and color with the promise of sun. Babies and small children wriggle, stretch, and cry. It is a cold, crisp morning. The smells of the ancient marsh, now free of water in the rainless season, ooze out of the Earth and waft their primordial scents and memories around the emerging consciousness of the new dawn. These memories are of dead or now extinct organisms, bushland and rain forest, of gullingi rains that soaked decomposing life-forms into the very fabric of the Earth to nourish new life. Birds warble up the daylight in a cacophony of news, heralding the day's winds, heat, and hunting.

The man straggles from his bedding and looks around. He looks around the camping area for signs of night visitors—a snake track or perhaps a goanna, dingo, or scavenger bird. These signs are noted and followed to the point where they disappear to ensure kin and children's safety. He drifts to the firepit mindful of the feel of the day, the look of the land, the sounds and smells of nature. Firewood is being broken into kindling by Granny who was the first to arise. Coals are stirred to flickering by the man and the fire is awakened to its rebirth. A new day is born as Daughter Sun and flames stir up their life-giving heat and power.

Grandmothers coo softly to the very young as they lift the little ones from their blankets in the early morning light as the fire flares. This is Wuudu Time, when Morning Star is absorbed into the eagerness of morning light, the time of awakening awareness. As Daughter Sun kindles the new day and the man kindles the flame of the campfire, awareness is kindled in the children of the tribe.

Hands are warmed over the flames. A grandmother touches a child's eyes with her warmed hands and whispers quietly, intimately "Eeh! You must share . . . you must not look around in other people's camps for things you want. Everything is there for you in the Wurnan." She warms her hands again, puts them on the sleepy child's nose and says "Eeh! You must not sniff around or beg for other people's food. Your food is here for you. You must hunt for your own food ... work hard in your lifetime." Then her hands touch the child's mouth and she exhorts "Eeh! You must not curse other people. You bring big shame to us if you curse them. They are our brothers and sisters, our aunts, our uncles ... they protect you in your place." Finally her hands move to the male child's pubic area, for example, as she says, "Eeh! You must not look at other womans. You have promise wife in Wurnan."

Families move gently to prepare food to begin the day. Everyone is reminded to fear the day. Fearing the day makes everyone alert, mindful of the multitude of actions and interactions that are happening constantly within the environment. Going about daily chores such as making toilet, gathering wood, boiling soup or tea, or shaking out the bedding has an inherent danger. Such activities undertaken mindfully mean that danger is lessened from the unexpected centipede under the sleeping rug, the snake that wakes with daylight, the log that hides the scorpion or spider, the wind that blows the fire out of the pit, the rain that dampens clothing or food. One is reminded to be mindful of the bough of the tree that falls, signifying an accident to a kinsman, or the bird whose cry tells of approaching weather, fish, or animal. Fearing the day means that the unexpected is embraced for its meaning so every event and sign becomes instructional in some way.

Parents and older siblings make sure that younger ones are fed while others share food and stories from the night. A mother dreams a snake, her son's Gi, the symbol of the Wunggud essence that named him. He and his family have been visiting another tribe and have been away for several months. A relation dreaming his Gi means that he is now returning to his own family. He recognizes that it is time to return because his sinews have grown weary. Before going to sleep that night he yawns, sending the sign to his own family that he is coming back. His mother receives the message of the yawn in her dream of his Gi symbol. The family will now prepare for his return with great excitement.

Dreams and visions are told, considered privately, and usually noted without comment. Foretellings of the right actions are shared, learned through Wunggud enactments in the visceral world of unconsciousness, that portal of the universe that opens wide in order to be transversed with uncritical, uncluttered clarity. Dream is the medium in which ancestors and messengers of Wunggud infuse insight and knowledge to their peoples. There are no lies in the dreamworld. Dreaming surrenders its fulsome knowledge and wisdom in the absence of consciousness.

This day the women gather their digging sticks, twine, baskets, and children ready for fishing and hunting for goanna, sugarbag or wild honey, long-neck turtle, lily roots, berries, and yams. The brun-brun or kingfisher bird has sung its story about abundance in the river. There are fish waiting to surrender themselves to the women to feed their families. The bird is named to mean "woman's digging stick" because she is long and straight and nests deep in the riverbank. In this secret place, inside the womb of the Earth connected to the life-giving waters of the river, the brun-brun bird is a reflection of woman. She digs into her nest like a woman's digging stick.

Along the winding track through the bush en route to the water's edge, the women and children chatter as they collect food, sometimes pausing while they root yams from their deep burrows with their digging sticks. It is a difficult operation and the young girls sometimes break the brittle yam stems that lead to the roots. Food is carried in bark baskets made by old women who teach younger ones these skills and crafts. Older women draw the children's attention to nature as it emerges in their pathway. Insects, grasses, bushes, trees, birds, reptiles, and animals are all named to the young—named in their own right and in their relationship to the children. There is an order to the natural world into which all of existence fits, including humans.

Naming and providing the language of the world is mostly Women's Business because women are the primary caregivers to the prepubescent young. Because nature is essentially Wunggud in action, the world is named as a series of actions that, when linked together, generate a whole image or picture. This is the pattern of life or Wurnan system, the intricate ecology of sacred relationships.

Small digging sticks are made for the children so they can imitate their mothers in the search for goanna or digging for yams and other bulbs, or to defend themselves in case of accidental danger such as stepping on a snake. Mothers and aunts teach by example and children learn by imitation. Berries, edible or medicinal stalks, barks, roots, leaves, grubs, ants, and other insects are collected, tasted, and eaten immediately.

On arrival at the fishing place, the women choose their positions along the bank of the river between the pandanas, each throwing a pebble in the water to wake up the fish grazing lazily among the lilies. Children entertain themselves unsupervised, climbing, making gings to shoot at small birds, whittling sticks, telling stories, swimming, or fishing.

A young child playfully whacks another child on the head with his digging stick. There is a yelp of pain and copious tears. Mothers shriek, laugh, and exclaim at the incident while the wounded child is quickly removed from the scene to avoid further attack. The offending child stands mute, digging stick still in hand. Knowing that this child has not yet reached the age of change of teeth, and does not have the maturity to understand the danger of his action, a mother warns him gently "Aahee! You better look out or big crocodile will come and get you!" and hands him over to a young girl whose first teeth are already being replaced by her maturity teeth. He is not punished for his action by his mothers yet he realizes that he has done something that might have raised the interest of a Wunggud crocodile or spirit which might sneak up and get him. He finds another activity.

Later, when his second teeth come through, he will be told the story of Dumby, the Law Owl who was persecuted and tortured by two young boys. He will hear that the boys were told not to mess with the Owl while the parents were away hunting for the day. These boys got bored that particular day, however, and, seeing Dumby sitting in the tree, threw rocks at him to bring him down. This owl is a Sacred Owl, representing the Law. It is forbidden to hurt or kill him. But the boys decided to have a bit of fun so they tortured Dumby by plucking out his feathers. The Owl was unable to escape so he suffered the boys' taunts and injuries. Once they plucked him of his feathers and freedom, the boys threw Dumby into the air to see if he could fly but the Owl fell crashing to the ground. So the boys picked some spinifex sticks, poked them into him, threw him into the air again, and again he fell to the ground. More spinifex and spear grass were stuck into the poor bird, again he was thrown up in the air, and again and again he fell down. Dumby grew weak as he endured the torture, unable to get away from the laughing boys. He was hurled up into the air once more but this time he did not fall to the ground. This time he flew to a rock shelf where a Wandjina lived. Dumby told Wandjina the story of what the boys had done. The Wandjina was extremely angry and called a meeting of all the other Wandjina in the land. They collected at a meeting place, traveling from all directions—north, south, east, and west. They discussed the behavior of the boys and, in their extreme anger at the Law Owl's treatment, summoned their powers to generate a wild whirlwind. The wind's vortex created quicksand in the ground into which everyone in the tribe was sucked. Everyone, that is, except one boy and one girl. These two young children jumped into the pouch of a kangaroo who hopped them away. Because of his suffering, Dumby dissolved himself into the rock face and became a painting.

Back at the river's bank, the baskets fill with fish. A campfire is prepared, food cooked and shared among the women and children. A young girl gets a fishbone stuck in her throat. As one old woman removes the bone and attends the little girl, another mother picks up a stick and beats the child's mother. She has not been looking after her child properly. She has not been a mindful mother. This is the latest in a number of incidents resulting from neglect so now she is punished just as all the parents in the tribe were punished to death by Wandjina for not training the boys in proper respect of the Law and the Owl. Parents are punished for the lawlessness of their children as well as for accidents or misadventures suffered by those for whom they are responsible.

It is a hunting day for the men too. The hunting party collects tools and equipment and leaves early. Today they are not going very far in their search for food because they have younger boys with them who will tire early. Bush tucker is abundant at this time of year and they know the women are fishing. With spears, axes, and knives they set off in single file. As they move away from the camp they fall into a rhythm of mindful, silent walking, watching for any sign that will tell them of game—a sudden movement of birds, the particular call of another, the appearance of fresh droppings.

After a long walk one of the hunters sights a bush turkey, a Busbee, feeding in the distance, almost indistinguishable from the surrounding vegetation. The hunting party splits, moving stealthily upwind to surround the bird. As they close on their quarry two initiated young men burst into a run, wielding their spears. The others act as a barricade, ready to herd the big bird toward the spear throwers as it tries to escape. The spears are thrown, the bird is winged and runs amok. All the men chase and herd until another spear is successfully landed and the bird drops. The hunter whose spear lands the death-blow lifts the bird to his shoulders and hangs it around his neck. They move on.

Firewood is collected as they approach the lagoon where they will make their lunch camp. Some men prepare the fire and the bird while others go to the waterhole to dive for freshwater crocodile and turtle or to swim. Young, uninitiated boys are shown how to recognize broken foliage, tracks or scratches in the ground, and the behavior of animals. They collect sugarbag and the boys are warned that they must not take all of it. Some must be left or they will be punished by Agula, the devil spirit. In early times a boy disobediently returned to a tree where wild honey had been collected. He put his hand in the hole to get the last of it. The third time he put his hand inside it got stuck in the sticky sugarbag. His parents heard him calling out and when they reached him they found his hand firmly glued in the hole. He was reminded that he had been told not to finish off the honey, that he must leave some behind, that Agula would punish him. The boy was able to get his hand out only after his father sang a magic song to release him. He was very sorry for doing what he was told was forbidden.

The bush turkey is plucked, slit, and gutted. The guts are thrown into the fire for immediate eating along with yams and any fish that might have been caught. The turkey is cut up according to rules that govern who will receive specific parts of the bird and then cooked. Some is eaten immediately while the legs and ribs are carried back to camp to be shared with the old men, women, and children. Sometimes goanna, turtle, and other foods are forbidden to the young boys because they are in training for their initiation. They are not allowed any fat because it is believed this will make their genitals grow fatty and weak. They will not grow as strong hunters if they are weak in their manhood.

Song, joy, and laughter ripple through the group of men and boys as they eat their lunch with each one recounting his experience of the day's hunting. Soon they extinguish the fire and at midafternoon they return to camp to be greeted by their kin.

For the young boys who accompany the men in their hunting pursuits, it is a privilege and a sign that they are soon to be prepared for initiation. During this time many foods will become taboo and they will start their training in the behaviors and protocols that befit an initiated male. The young boy has to learn about his relationship with every other member of the tribe, his Gi symbols, taboos in diet, behaviors, and relationships. He is being prepared to leave the secure embrace of the women's world for his manhood training and responsibilities.

The women return to camp by early afternoon on this day. Children play around the camp, swim in the waterhole, and eat food that has been gathered during the morning. Mothers sit in groups on the ground in the shade of a tree, making or repairing baskets, fishnets, hooks, or grinding roots, barks, leaves, and nuts for medicines, all the while singing the songs of the land, the food, and the ancestors who have provided them. Some take pandanas and cycad fruit to the water's edge. Here the fruits are placed in a twine cage for soaking, a three- or four-day process that leaches out their toxins. Others grind and powder the already prepared fruits ready for making bread.

That evening, as the families sit around to share food, a tired infant starts to cry vigorously, and in a temper tantrum throws his food at his aunt. Although only two years old, he is a good shot, hitting her in the face and chest with the soggy pulp. Not satisfied with one handful, he fills another hand and hurls its contents, hitting his target again. Without moving from their places, the mothers chide the child gently warning, "Eeh! What are you doing! That big emu will come for you. Look out, he's just over there watching you. See him watching? You better watch out or he'll come for you!"

Nobody chastises, punishes, or in any way attempts to *directly* stop the child's behavior. He is simply warned that Wunggud will cause something to happen to him and he is then distracted by suckling or is given something else to amuse him.

After eating and telling stories from the day, an old man starts tapping the ceremony sticks and singing. Soon he is joined by others, and some older men and women get up and dance the stories that belong with the songs. They are joined by boys and girls, and even the very young, all singing and dancing in celebration of the end of another day in which Wandjina and the Harvest Spiritmen have provided them with plenty of food.

Ngarinyin children grow up without direct, authoritative command. From early childhood to prepubescence, socialization comes from within and according to the laws of nature. This is the Law. The biological process of maturation provides physical signposts to herald the level of awareness that a child can incorporate. Prior to the emergence of teeth, babies are held most of the time. As a baby's focus shifts from the immediate world to follow sounds, smells, and resonances more distant, these are named in terms of their action and place in Creation.

The emergence of first teeth usually heralds the child's movement from the arms of kinsfolk to the ground. Now crawling, he follows his curiosity about the textures, tastes, and comforts that lie beyond direct human contact. First teeth indicate a readiness for naming the world with language, the beginning of awareness of identity. As these impermanent teeth increase, so does the vista of experience. The world's actions are named, its influences identified, its relationships imprinted on the young child. These are reinforced in story, song, and dance in which the very young are free to participate in their innocent self-assurance. They can do no wrong because awareness of wrongdoing requires knowledge of the Law and the ability to apply that knowledge to personal conduct.

The Ngarinyin believe that awareness does not emerge until the child's first teeth start to fall out, and the new, strong, deeply rooted permanent teeth poke through. This transition, a physical death and rebirth, signifies the passage from toddlerhood, with its absolute dependence on others, to a new independence wherein the child can forage mindfully for himself. He can now learn to apply the knowledge absorbed in his life's experiences to new situations as values and principles. In other words, his ability to absorb abstract principles of behavior is now considered grounded in the deep roots of his second teeth, symbols of his personal power. He becomes responsible for his own actions and their consequences in Wunggud.

At the time of the change of teeth, it is enough to warn a child who breaks the Law, "Hey, be careful what you do. Remember Dumby!" Wrong behavior continues to be regarded as miscreance that needs correction rather than punishment. Parents and families will watch a group of children eat an entire picnic of food in a sitting and shake their heads as if saying, "Aah! Wunggud will do something to them for sure."

When a young person has been well taught, he knows that his choice of action will resonate, or not, with the power of Wunggud. His rooted second teeth ground him in that power, uniting him with all of life in Wunggud. He is encouraged to understand and let his behavior reflect the meaning of the principles, parables, stories he has been taught not in an analytic way but through the use of mythic imagery. He will be warned that certain actions are wrong actions, that they do not sustain the pattern of life. The warning will be reinforced indirectly through story, but the choice of action will be his own. He will not be stopped from proceeding in a wrong action. Wunggud will give him the teaching he needs in another way, at another time. If he falls out of a tree and breaks his leg, gets bashed up by other boys, or gets caught in the water lilies, he is reminded of his choice of wrong action and that Wunggud has punished him.

When accident or injury falls on a wrongdoer, mother will say, even if it is days later, "You did that bad thing before. Now look what has happened to you." Behaviors are always linked to the powers of the Law, not to the authority of man.

If accident or injury befalls a child through persistent parental neglect, the parent or caregiver may be punished in front of the child and family. This reflects the Dumby story which assumes that if children are not properly taught the Law misadventure results and because children are innocent parents are punished for their failure to conduct themselves properly as Law teachers. When a child sees his mother receive a thrashing because he committed a wrongdoing against a living creature, another human, or the Law, it is considered a deterrent because no child wants to see his mother punished as a result of his actions. He is shamed and sorry and is expected to modify his actions in the future or else his mother will suffer again.

There is no such thing as guilt in Ngarinyin society. Shaming is the great punishment. It is the public broadcasting that certain actions against a person, an animal, a site, a relationship, a Law, or taboo have caused great shame not only to a particular individual but to the miscreant's whole family and even the entire tribe. There is no greater punishment or sorrow than shaming. A shamed young person finds it almost impossible to hold his head up. Shaming is followed by "I'm sorry" behaviors, not apologies but actions. As these behaviors continue, they are embraced over time by all those affected and the child's head gradually lifts. There are no words of condemnation, no attitudes that generate guilt, no threats, and no corporal punishment. In fact, no words or actions will remind the miscreant of his offensive conduct. It is past, gone and forgotten by all. After shaming, reacceptance signifies forgiveness and this is absolute.

From birth, separation is a key feature and a normal state for Western children. Inside Western homes, rooms are divided by walls and doors and each room has a function and a label. Bedrooms for sleeping are separated from each other. The kitchen, playroom, family room, laundry, den, garage have their own distinctive furnishings and function and require their own special customary behavior. Bedroom behavior is different from kitchen, laundry, or family room behavior. In addition to room behaviors there are ownership or proprietary patterns within each. There is often Dad's corner chair, Mom's chair and drawers, a locked liquor cabinet for which Dad has the key, cushions on the floor for children. Adults never use these cushions except on weekends when Dad chills out enough to get down there with the kids for a wrestle or game.

When a baby gets teeth it gets mobile. This is the time when a child is effectively domesticated. The primary domestication values are relationship with property and possessions, and the individual rights of ownership. Because of this, competition and independence are encouraged before a child can walk or talk. Children learn that there is "Mommy's bedroom" and "Johnny's bike," "your toys" and "my books." The ownership of possessions endows rights of use and access and there are rules and disciplines relating to use and rights within every room of the home. By the time a child can walk or talk he has learned hundreds of detailed protocols, conventions, and customs that relate to property, material culture, its ownership rules, maintenance, and use. Most infancy and childhood discipline relates to the development and maintenance of these material values.

Western children learn that dirt has its very own mystique with specific and various rules related to its appearance and disappearance. They become knowledgeable about the various special cleaning agents that relate to specific surfaces—toothpaste cleans tooth porcelain but not the washbasin, the oven interior requires a different cleaner than the fridge interior, and windows, carpets, sinks, the toilet, grease spots, walls, and furniture each have their own special cleansing agent.

As the child moves into the toddler stage, he moves beyond the boundaries of house and home to day care, other people's homes, and to the park for fresh air and exercise. "Outside" is a place of high adventure and lurking danger. Within the home's boundaries nature is more or less under control. Any animals or insects caught trespassing are quickly disposed of with powders, sprays, and swats. The family garden is usually contained and controlled in patterns of safety and beauty, generally maintained by father and detailed by mother. The local park is similar with the additional delights of plastic, wood, and steel activity centers.

A child's first outing to the bush must be an extraordinary experience. In fact the natural bushland usually increases the parents' anxiety and watchfulness because they are unfamiliar with its ecology, food potential, and inhabitants. In nature, everything is out of control yet exciting for a curious, adventurous child. He is taught to stay within the safe boundaries of cleared car parks, grassed patches, and walking tracks and not to venture off these for fear of being bitten, stung, or cut. While independence is fostered in the house, out in the natural world a toddler's independence is contained within the boundaries of parental familiarity and fear thresholds, all of which the child absorbs.

During these developmental years the child is introduced to the imaginal world through books and occasionally storytelling, although this is less common. The imaginal world contains animated animals, plants, houses, fruits and vegetables, tools and machines who think and talk. Through the story, the Western child develops a basic understanding of ethics, morality, and family and community values. It is an exciting, wondrous world which is recreated in play, through painting and drawing, dress up, constructing with blocks, counting, classifying, and sharing.

By the age of four, the emphasis begins to shift from the imaginary world of make-believe and stories to the practical skills of mathematics and language. The child begins to learn about truth and lies, fact and fantasy, reality and imagination. The rich, textured world of myth gradually gives way to the solid-state world of fact, reason, and classification which are the intellectual, rational, logical, and controlling building blocks of Western cultural life. The child's intellectual development soon overtakes its creative and imaginal development. Now instead of applying color randomly to a page, the child is rewarded for drawing something real like a truck, face, animal, or action. Instead of making plastic blocks into an unrecognizable sculpture, he is praised for sorting by color, size, or number.

Father Christmas, the Easter Bunny, and the Tooth Fairy still visit but few children know their origins or the significance of the rituals because the spiritual intent has been absorbed by the doctrine of consumerism.

Western children are raised primarily by their mothers who conduct this occupation largely on their own without the support of a collective of women other than that which they arrange on a social basis. She is the person with whom the child establishes a deep bond of trust because she not only provides for her child's every need but interprets the world and gives meaning to it. Because children have limited and regulated exposure to other adults, the ties that bind are hers.

Fathers play a supportive role after work and on weekends. Mothers conduct the family relationships with schools, children's friends, sports participation, and family health maintenance. They deliver most of the discipline, calling on their husbands when reinforcement is needed.

For father, family time is usually restricted so children must compete with each other, mother, and television for his attention. Contact time with his children tends to be practical and action oriented. He wants to measure achievements, skills, and performance, sometimes comparing his child's development with the rate and pace of other children. He is usually the more distant observer of process and progress within the family while wanting his children to be advanced, in the top half, the football or basketball player who lands the winning goal. The seed of competitiveness is firmly sown through this relationship and internalized by children, then taken on as a value into school.

At school the real, measurable world is presented to children predominantly by books supplemented by direct and hands-on experience. Education is based on the scientific method with its values of logic and reason, the observed and classified, the evidentiary and concrete. Life is presented through subjects like health, social studies, science, music, and art, all of which are underpinned by mathematics and language. Subjects with a scientific or language orientation have a much higher value than those of an imaginal and creative nature. The mythic, psychic, spiritual, imaginal and dream potential of children receives minimal attention or validation.

Life skills such as relationships within community, peer groups, family, nation, and environment are usually objectified and dealt with as "special extras," or as themes for a term. Ethics and morality, social and environmental responsibility, gender role and function, understanding psyche and feeling, contextual philosophy, ceremony and ritual, and the meaning of life, culture, and relationship are not considered school subjects and are all but missing from school curricula in Western education. Children learn these values unconsciously by absorption at home and from their social and recreational interactions. Because schooling reinforces those values considered important to the survival of the culture, Western children quickly learn that masculine values are not only superior to feminine values but that economic work performed by men is widely acknowledged while life skills work done by women is economically, and therefore psychologically, valueless or invisible. This perspective is internalized as the basis of their worldview.

Discipline is generally direct, often guilt based, individually centered, and usually relates specifically to the offense. Until the 1960s, corporal punishment at home and within schools was usual and effective. Since the 1980s most Western governments have introduced legislation that protects children from such punishment, expanding their jurisdiction to the governance of psychological punishment in accordance with a United Nations Convention on Rights of the Child.

Most offenses by children are against property, and they yield the harshest punishments both at home and within the state. At home the management and maintenance of material possessions is paramount. Neatness, tidiness, cleanliness within interior and exterior boundaries, the cleanliness of all surfaces, clothing, tools, utensils, and appliances are the primary focus of family discipline and therefore values. These values are inculcated into children from early childhood through adolescence and beyond. The concept of ownership is the earliest taught value. Possessions are related to the individual and his or her ownership of them, responsibility for them, and exclusive rights over them.

While prepubescent Western children are conditioned in the arts and skills of controlling their worlds, both material and natural, Ngarinyin children are conditioned in the arts and skills of relationship with and within theirs. By the age of eleven Western children are expected to be fully domesticated, literate, and numerate and to be able to communicate in coherent written language. They will probably have acquired sophisticated computing skills and be sufficiently comfortable with the function and use of money to participate in an urban, material world. Their major lessons in life have been to become considerate, self-confident, self-centered individuals who will compete against each other in all fields to get ahead. They have had limited exposure to and experience of the Mythic because the spiritual realm is given little real value within their culture and society. Ngarinyin children the same age are expected to be fully conversant with the relationship system, their place in it, and the protocols, ceremony, ritual, and taboos associated with the pattern of life in which they belong. They will have acquired competency in survival skills, be able to read the landscape, weather, navigate by the stars, and know the cycles of plants, seasons of growing, and behaviors of animals. Their major lessons in life have been to fear the day, become strong contributors to tribal life, and to uphold the Law of Wurnan, the pattern of sharing and their place in it. They have no real knowledge or understanding of ownership or individuality, linear measurement, or written language since their worldview is literal, rooted in stories and expressed in visual and performing arts. The two experiences are worlds apart.

Ngarinyin children today can only assimilate Western culture through their unique worldview. While many of their rich practices have now disappeared, the manner in which they interpret experiences, make judgments, and synthesize information reflects the traditional way. Consequently many children experience difficulties with academic scholarship and social interaction in mainstream society and education.

As this problem has only recently been recognized by Australian public institutions the development of a strategic response is still in its infancy. However, in 1994 a number of private institutions and individuals, in collaboration with Ngarinyin families, embarked on a cocultural education initiative that reflects the worldviews of both Ngarinyin and Western cultures.

Christina Kennedy

Lukie Mowaljarlai, a few days before making the long journey south to Guildford Grammar School in Perth, holding the bush turkey shot by his grandfather during Bush University.

Chapter Four

Metamorphosis

Adolescence

Twelve Whitefellas attend the first Bush University deep in Ngarinyin country at the Marunbabidi Wunggud waterhole. One of the visitors is a nineteen-year-old girl who comes with her father who is a judge. An athletic, vibrant, and fun-loving young woman who loves outdoor activities, she launches into every experience with great enthusiasm. Two young teenage Ngarinyin boys are enchanted by her. They follow her around, accidentally bumping her, splashing her in the waterhole, telling her stories and anecdotes that make her laugh, and their hearts sing. I can see trouble, and warn her that their fathers may get upset because the boys are in their taboo years when they must stay away from young women. She understands and tries to avoid them or make sure she is not alone with them. They are not so easily dissuaded. Still they flirt and follow, until one morning around the campfire, the father of one of the boys calls me over. His eyes are as dark as his mood. I can feel his saltiness as he says, "You got to tell that girl to stay away from these boys. They not allowed to sniff around her—they know that. She's taboo. They'll get a flogging if they keep mucking around her. They got to learn too much before they get around with girls." I am growled at because I am the guardian of the Whitefellas. The young woman actively avoids them, even avoiding eye contact and conversation, for the duration of her time in their country. The boys now lower their heads whenever she is around. Now that the taboos are observed by both black and white, cordiality is resumed.

The song of the ancestral Harvest Spiritmen greeted this fine, early cool-season day. Knock-em-down rains had recently flattened the meters-tall spear grasses, making movement in the country easier and increasing visibility. Everyone had been waiting for these rains and knew they were due because the green of the grass stalks had withdrawn to below knee height like long socks when they sag, a sure forecast that the heavy, sharp storms that follow the northward journey of the Big Wet would hit soon. Once the grasses were knocked down and dried out, the country could be burned.

When the sun set on the previous evening everybody saw a group of clouds formed in the shape of men hanging in the sky, calling the people to hunting and gathering. They knew the cloud formation was the sign of the Harvest Spiritmen telling them that plenty of food was available here and now. So this morning they sang the song of the two Spiritmen who walked the land like Wandjina and lived well off Earth's great harvest.

Burning the country is always exciting because there are so many animals hiding in the grasses, big and fat after the rich, green grazing of the rain time. Everyone is excited about today's hunt. Small children will be left at the camp with the grandmothers because burning can be dangerous to little ones who have not yet learned to respect the power and heat of a shifting fire. People will be chasing animals too and they don't want their hunt hampered by children. The children are happy in the camp because the grandmothers sing the old songs, and tell stories of ancient times, of Creation time and Lai Lai when all the world came into being, when the ancestors roamed the Earth putting everything in its place.

This hunt is a special one because two boys are preparing for their initiation and big groups of Lawpeople are beginning to arrive from neighboring tribes and lands. Fresh food has to be added to the great store of yams, breads, and sugarbag that will feed the people who are coming to participate in the ceremony that conducts the boys into manhood. Men, women, and children who have traveled hundreds of miles to celebrate and welcome the boys into full tribal status as initiated young men arrive hungry and tired from their journeys.

All through the Big Wet the two boys visited each of the surrounding tribal lands to introduce themselves and to invite their distant kinsmen to receive them at their initiation. That journey was a test of the boys' strength and endurance, their ability to survive on the skills they had learned, the quality of their years of instruction and training, and the diligence of their own kinsmen as teachers and navigators. It required great self-discipline and absolute obedience to the Lawmen who accompanied them and whom they had to serve during the traveling months. These months had been a time of fasting and discipline for the two initiates.

Ever since their parents and uncles noticed that the boys had reached puberty, the boys have been on a special regimen of food, observances, taboos, and instruction. They learned how to make spears, woomera, digging sticks, and axes, how to track animals and fish for black bream in the waterholes and barramundi in the rivers and sea. They had participated in kangaroo hunts but in this taboo time did not hunt kangaroo themselves nor eat the fat of any animal, reptile, or bird. Such food might make their genitals soft and spongy, their sperm weak, and their children sickly or deformed. They learned the painted pattern of their own Gi symbols, their dances and songs, and have been painted up in white ochre only. They know that the powerful red ochre, the blood of the kangaroo, is reserved for older, initiated men.

Once while hunting with his uncles, aunts, grandmothers, and other young people on a picnic, a young girl brought water from the lagoon for them all to share. Before one of the initiates drank any of the water brought by this girl, his grandmother poured some of it on her hands and rubbed it on his forehead and cheeks. Another time, hunting had been successful and the men caught a big kangaroo. The initiate was not allowed to eat any of it because he was permitted to eat kangaroo caught only by certain men and on this day, the successful hunter was not one of those men. Instead he ate fish and yam.

Everybody was ready, the songs sung and the tools, spears, and baskets prepared. Blessed by the Harvest Spiritmen the group set off. The party moved swiftly and quietly, men and boys separate from women and girls, all focused on the rhythm of their steps as they headed through the trees and newly knocked-down grass. The older men selected a place to begin the burning. Noting the density of grass, the distance from escape routes for animals and man, wind direction and strength, the freshness and type of animal tracks on the ground, and the messages of birds, they paused to plan their burning strategy. The men would chase kangaroo, emu, and bush turkey while the women and girls would chase smaller game such as bandicoot, go-anna, or possum.

They want a low, cold fire, not one that will get away or rise into the tree canopy. If the wind is too strong they cannot burn the country today. But it is not. A gentle breeze licks them in the morning heat, just right for a manageable burn. The Harvest Spiritmen were, as always, right to alert them to the correctness of time, place, and opportunity. Older men set fire to the grasses in an arc which forms a semicircle. This forces the animals into a narrower escape route. A group of men remain behind the fire line, following it, watching for sudden move-ment. In a clearing ahead of the fire the other hunters, with their spears ready, are waiting for the fleeing kangaroo, emu, and bush turkey. Meanwhile the women follow the fire still further behind, chasing and catching their quarry, slower moving and smaller. Goanna and bandicoot surrender to the sticks and dogs of the women hunters, their lives given for the maintenance of the pattern of life and the ecology of relationship.

At the camp the grandmothers and mothers who stayed to care for young children set about preparing the ceremonial food. Sugarbag and yam must be readied for the sacred initiation ceremony which will culminate in the ritual circumcision of the boys. They must scrupu-lously sift the sugarbag for any foreign bodies—bark, insects, dirt, wax—so that the honey is a clean, pure, light liquid, the nectar of the Earth Mother who is about to receive the blood of her two sons. This honey must not be touched by women's hands. It is gathered from a tree's interior with sticks twirled around like spaghetti, placed in a bark bucket, then filtered into a special bladder. In this way the honey retains its own Earth Mother energy and does not absorb the energy, taste, or smell of the women. Its purity determines the purity of will and spirit of the tribe, and the strength and destiny of the initiates. When it is ready, the bladder is hung on a tree branch to be cooled by wind and shade.

For the women of the tribe this is a time of great grief and immense pride and joy. They know that the boys are leaving them, leaving the Motherworld that has sustained and trained them to be strong men. They sing the songs of loss for their sons to the man's world from which they will return not as young boys but as young men of the tribe, named and inscribed in their full status and place in Wurnan.

When everybody has arrived, the celebrations begin. Every evening is filled by dancing and singing the reenactments of Creation, the songs of the ages which call up the Earth's energies and celebrate the union of belonging in this timeless land and its cycles of birth, transformation, and death.

The boys are taken from their families by the Lawmen. Mothers and grandmothers weep, wailing their grief, loss, and fear for the survival of their sons. In the distance is the Men's Business ground, a taboo place for women marked by an invisible barrier over which no woman or child may step for fear of great wrath, tribal shame, and the curse of illness or even death. Women can go up to this energetic line to pass along the ritual food of purified honey and carefully prepared yam, bread, and water, and then return to their circle of power where they conduct their ceremony and songs in this ritual and celebrate their place in the pattern of life. They recall in song the gift of their children, their totem and smoking ceremonies, the suckling, growth, and lessons in survival skills, the language, myth, and meanings that these boys were taught while in the primary care of mothers and grandmothers. They call on the spirits of the Earth, nature, their ancestors, Wunggud, and Wandjina to give their sons courage and strength, the ability to endure their destiny, and this ritual passage to manhood.

In the Men's Business ground the chanting begins. There is a ring around the moon, a sign to all the world that boys are being initiated. The Songmaster is surrounded by initiated men, painted and decorated in totemic symbols of tassles, armbands, and head pieces given to them by the Guyon Guyon. This is the bird who pecked Wunggud's gifts of stone tools and ceremonial dress into the caves and rock shelters as painted images or communiqués from the Divine. The men, who come from near and far, dance the whole of Creation into being to bear witness to this rite. At the circle's center are the young men who are encircled with the hair belts that bind them to the land and their tribe. Each song is accompanied by tapping sticks, chanting, and the dances that represent every totemic reptile, bird, fish, and frog of their country, calling up all ancestral spirits in the land to be present at the initiation. The singing and dancing continue for days so the Lawmen can be sure every creature is present, that all nature bears witness to the consecration of their sons to the Law. Even blue-tongued lizard is welcomed in song in remembrance of the first initiation. She performs the special role of creating the pathway for initiation by rolling over and over to form a track along which the boys will pass into the tribe.

When the whole of Creation is energetically present, the resonance of the Earth is palpable. The men form a line and the boys are hoisted up to lie facing the heavens across the backs of their kin, their arms locked through their fathers' arms. This is the sacrificial passage between before and after, heaven and Earth, boyhood and manhood, the mother's world and man's world. Days of singing and dancing have created an exquisite, rarefied atmosphere, a vortex of power within the ceremony area. Before sunup, in the subtle pink light of dawn, the men sing the song of Becoming. One man climbs the tree of initiation to gather the leaves that, when spread, will form the tableau on which the final act will be executed. The men of the tribe sing, panting "Yeah!" as each step of the climb is mastered. The leaves are dropped to those who will gather them and put them in position. When the tableau is ready, the boys' brothers-in-law lie face up on the leaves. The boys are laid over their bodies, also face up, their legs held by the legs of their brothers-in-law who also grasp them tightly under their arms. The boys' torsos are extended and exposed to their destiny and the rite of manhood. The chanting continues—haunting and compelling—as the men sing up the dawn and the birth of the new young men. The boys are cut, their flesh and blood spilling into the Earth as a sacrifice in sacred consecration of the place where they belong, the renewal of the tribe in the land to which they are now biologically joined.

In the distance the shrill wailing of women splits open the dawn's quiet, releasing the Earth's receptive power to embrace the blood of her sons, the newly consecrated men of the tribe.

The initiated young men are immediately smoked in the fire which seals their awakening to manhood. Then they are anointed with ash to promote rapid, safe healing. When their bleeding subsides they are walked around. Then they sleep.

Not only are the boys passed from their mothers' care into manhood, but they are also passed from their fathers' care to the care of other older men—uncles, brothers, and grandfathers. One of these will stay with the young men in their healing time until the final act of this long ceremony is undertaken. The new young men spend several weeks of solitude with their caretaker and teacher to consolidate their new life. When the healing is complete, the young men are embraced in a final ritual smoking ceremony which confirms their strength, resolve, and responsibility to their people and land.

Before Western influence, this ceremony marked the beginning of seven years of strict discipline, rules, and training. During this time they develop their skills in survival and endurance through mindfully taking risk, seeking adventure, and confronting death. Under the tutelage of the older men, they learn to use spears in real hunting that before now they have been permitted to simply replicate and imitate. There are many more taboos to observe and responsibilities to absorb. As they mature into full manhood they must not meet or mess around with women or girls. They have a promise wife ready for them, and until their forearm hair grows strong and their whiskers change from soft down to stubble they are taboo for all sexual liaison. Their emerging male energy and sexual passions must be released through other action. They can run, chase, hunt, climb, walk, compete, play-fight, and participate in all adult male activities with vigor and enthusiasm but they must not spill their seed with a woman while they are maturing. Any child born of immature seed might be inherently weak, a liability to the tribe and a shame to their identity.

As they mature and learn to redirect their sexual energies into skills and endeavors that benefit the whole group, their teachers know they must learn about womanhood and woman's power. At the age of maturity, the young men are initiated into the mysteries of woman in a rite involving an older widow. The young men are told to learn from this experience because it will be a part of their lives until they are old men. Through this rite, they are taught to fear and respect the power of woman and to adhere to the Laws of Wurnan through which they have a promise wife for whom they must wait and to whom they must be always faithful.

All Ngarinyin girls are promised to their husband at birth. By the time a girl reaches adolescence, the time when her menstruation commences, she knows she will soon have to fulfill this promise and stay with him. When she was born, her father placed her in the lap of her promise husband, committing her to him when the right time comes. Until then, her promise husband visited regularly, always bringing her family gifts of meat, shells, and spear points for her father to signify his goodness and dedication to the promise. Now, as her womanhood emerges, her mothers, aunts, and grandmothers train her in the arts and skills of looking after her husband and children. She knows that she will be leaving her family's camp and relocating to her promise husband's camp many miles away. This is her destiny, enshrined in the Law of Wurnan.

Being born of a Djingun father and Wodoi mother, she and her extended family are all Djingun, the skin group signifying the dust people whose sacred totem is a bird called the owlet nightjar. Her mother comes from the bone people whose totem is the spotted nightjar. Soon she will take her place with the bone people, carrying her Djingun Law with her and entrusting it to her husband and his people. Her children will be of the Wodoi skin group like their father. That is the way it is in the Law. But for now she is still in training, still ripening and living happily with her parents, siblings, and kinsmen.

When her menstrual life commences, her entry into full Women's Business is celebrated with the women's private ritual of Becoming. The transition from girl to woman is acknowledged by all who know her but especially by the menfolk. Her father and brothers immediately adopt their obligatory taboo behaviors. She can no longer talk with young men, and her fathers and uncles accord her the full respect of womanhood. She remains in the company of women only, forbidden to conduct any liaisons, participate in play, or be alone with boys or men. She is gradually given responsibilities and trained in the healing arts, medicine preparation, child care, food preparation and dietary taboos, women's song cycles, and women's Law. It is a joyous time lasting several years but always there is the knowledge that it will end.

It is coming up to full moon time, that glorious period when everyone in the camp is filled with laughter, dance, and song. She has been told that the Ri spirits—the spirit children in the Wunggud water—and the ancestral spirits dance and flicker around the sleeping group. Visible to the older people who recognize and acknowledge them, the Ri sometimes bear messages in dreams and sometimes become pranksters, creating mischief in and around the camp. She has seen their presence herself, rising out of the swamp like fireflies to waft and play in the primordial memories released from the Earth. It is as if all the world turns its face upward to the full moon as he travels across the night sky.

As the full moon comes and goes, she and many of the women in her camp also wax and wane in its rhythm, their menstrual cycles attuned to its phases. At full moon the young women feel their passions and energy bursting with life, love, and laughter. They know that like the seeds in the ground they are ripe for fertilization so their faces and the faces of flowers turn upward to receive the Ri. But this young woman is not yet ready for this step because her body is not quite ripened. Her nipples are still darkening, not yet the full, rich tone of maturity that will signify that her pelvic bones are big and strong enough to easily bear a child. She is therefore still taboo because she and her family do not want her to experience that difficult birthing so characteristic of the unripened woman.

As the moon starts its waning, the women's energies subside and they turn inward to prepare for their bleeding time in the moon's full darkness. At this time, the women go to their special place knowing that menstrual blood is too powerful and dangerous for the menfolk. A man may not touch, smell, or see the blood of the womb for fear of his very life. He is in mortal danger if he is careless at this woman's time.

The women quietly leave the camp, making sure that no drips fall where a man might walk, and move to a taboo place where their blood spills into the Earth, nourishing it with the bond of eternal motherhood. They and the Earth share this cycle subject to the ebb and flow of the tides of life.

The young woman goes with them. They lay out their bark bedsheets ready for the night, light their campfire, share the yams, sugarbag, goanna, berries, and lily roots they gathered on the way, and sing the celebratory songs of the Earth in exquisite unity with the power of nature embodied in their cycle. This precious few days of sharing joins the women in an exclusive, collective women's consciousness, away from the distractions and rigors of camp life. The breeding women menstruate together. Later, when they pass their child-bearing time, their cycle reverses as it does when they are suckling very young children.

She is told by the women that she must go to her promise husband's camp two moons hence. She must stay with his people for a time, to consolidate the vow made by her father at her birth. Her promise husband is an old man but gentle and good. He has been an excellent provider over the years and has been faithful to the Law. She has been well trained to look after him and must learn to take her place in the Wodoi world and Law. She doesn't really want to go but knows that she is unable to refuse.

Wurnan is maintained by her marriage because she not only takes her Djingun Law with her but takes the land that named her for his custody and stewardship. He marries her land and people as well and must serve them as a husband serves his wife. Thus the warp and weft of the land is woven into tribal life through the obligatory and tightly crafted relationship and marriage system.

Prior to Western influence the metamorphosis from puberty to womanhood was a much less public affair than the initiation of boys to manhood. There was no great gathering of the tribes, no weeks-long ceremony, and no dramatic ritual such as circumcision. Instead of breaking out into the world community as men do, girls were encouraged to go inward to the collective psyche of woman. Their transformation is quieter because it is not a reenactment of death and birth. Their physical change does not need to be publicly signified in ceremony because their bodies transform themselves. The acknowledgment of their transformation was as far-reaching as that for the males but significantly more subtle.

In Ngarinyin cosmology, male and female initiation into adulthood and sexual maturity is defined by physiology and biological function. The men's ritual acknowledges the importance of erection and ejaculation, the rigidity and force of nature in the action of insemination. The removal of the foreskin and the spilling of blood into the Earth is the action that binds men to their land. They nourish the land with their own flesh and blood and join their manhood to the reproductive power in and of Wunggud. Wunggud powerfully manifests itself in the male function of bursting and scattering seed. Women reflect the female function of the Earth. They spill their blood to nourish and sustain Earth's ability to provide food and the seeds of succession. Like the female in nature, women are fertilized from burst and scattered dream and seed according to the laws of genetic diversity. Women's maturation is an inward process during which their womb is cyclically prepared to receive the male's seed which it will accept or reject. These biological realities determine both the ritual and behaviors of men and women.

In Western culture many early adolescent girls stumble into the bloom of their womanhood because nothing in their society seems to acknowledge this passage. If they want to find out what is happening to them, they can turn to popular books and magazines for reference. More often than not, however, they talk with other girls whose metamorphosis is just as unacknowledged as their own. It is as if the changes in their bodies and minds are a secret. So they are often uninformed about the effects of the female hormones which are responsible for their physiological changes, their menstruation, and the development of a gender-specific view of the world and life. This transformation of mind and body receives no special recognition from society and no reflection in school curricula. Since genderlessness forms the fabric and substance of political and social policy, girls can be girls only at times of leisure or on weekends.

In their leisure time teenage girls are strongly influenced by the collective thinking of their female peers. They talk and talk, not just on weekends but often as soon as they get home from school. Their conversation and activities revolve around relationships, sexual forays, contraception, diet, well-being, romance, and ritual. They tentatively explore their maturation by evaluating what they observe in the adult world, compare the behaviors and attitudes of adults with how they feel and see things, and then adopt a corresponding code of values and conduct. Lately there's been an increase of interest in alternative healing, meditation, candles, aromatics, fairies, witches, charms, spells, and divination among teenage girls. Many also enjoy hard physical challenge and competition, intellectual sports, and academic success. But they are most curious about relationship, its nature and meaning.

They are intensely interested in gleaning, filtering, and finding language to fit the essence of their experiences and observations. Every nuance, every subtle action, interaction, feeling, or contrast between what they feel and what they intellectually rationalize and the drama of experience gains language and life in a confidential dialogue with a special friend or with peers. In this way, girls learn about intimacy, trust, betrayal, and the whole gamut of human emotion, a process that takes up hours and hours of leisure time. Girls discuss relationship on the telephone, at the beach, during school breaks, at the local deli or hangout place, and in the secrecy of bedrooms. This issue is the dominant subject and challenge for teenage girls everywhere in the Western world.

They are shy about sex yet sexually curious. Boys of the same age are usually regarded as immature so adult males take on a new and different role. Handsome, young male teachers are likely to be teased and flirted with by young emerging women and an older brother's friends are likely to be subtly targeted as testing material. Father is the safest one of all on which to practice being a gorgeous young woman because the teenager is still Dad's little girl. With him, she can safely flap her eyelashes, wiggle her bottom, and slink sensuously around his large frame to coyly ask for the car, permission to go out, or a pair of Doc Martins.

In most families, daughters are safe from predation and abuse by their fathers, uncles, and brothers. In too many, they are not. As parental authority is usurped by the state's assertion of its role as the guardian of morality, the primal parental urge to guide and protect the young is suffocated. Having been released from the responsibility to guide and respect their daughters and forfeiting the guidance of their sons to the state and its education system, some fathers, brothers, and uncles surrender to the power of their powerlessness and sexually abuse pubescent and adolescent daughters. With many social taboos virtually quashed in Western society and the increase of gender bending and sexual abuse, Western culture has come to resemble the declining Roman Empire.

A majority of Western girls have had their first full-blown sexual encounter by the time they reach their midteens. From the age of sixteen they can attend a doctor of their choice without a parent, be prescribed contraception, and are legally free to enjoy the sexual experiences life offers. Some mothers provide contraception to their sexually precocious daughters even earlier to ensure that they do not get caught with an unwanted pregnancy. Teenage sexuality is actively exploited in magazines and encouraged by peers. Virginity is no longer a presumed or desired state for marriage. Casual sex is common among teenage girls although its glamor diminishes after a couple of years. By the time adolescent young women reach full maturity, they have very often become discerning, even celibate, and may remain so until their mid- to late twenties. They learn that to get on in the world they need qualifications and a job, not marriage and children, so they postpone this part of their lives for as much as another decade or two.

Older women are notable by their absence in the lives of teenage girls. Very few adolescent girls are actively guided into womanhood by aunts and grandmothers. The reasons are as complex as they are diverse. Because school now plays such a significant role in adolescent life, the adults in a family are often superfluous. Many mothers and other significant females capitulate to popular social and political doctrine that asserts that youths have the same status and rights as mature adults. In the name of self-management and self-determination, modern parents are encouraged to respond softly and agreeably to their teenagers' needs and stages of maturity rather than guide or direct them. Extended families are no longer the cohesive units they once were, or even geographically or emotionally close. Any focus on gender differences or on any qualities that are unique to one gender or the other is not only politically incorrect, in many instances it is illegal. Many parents feel helpless to assume parental authority because they have little support in law. Some parents are just afraid of upsetting their teenage children for fear of losing them altogether. Perhaps a combination of some or all of these factors has discouraged older women from celebrating and guiding their daughters' journeys through adolescence to womanhood. Whatever an individual family's reasons, contemporary Western culture does not recognize the validity of parental authority or gender difference because it is a culture built on intellectual and not biological foundations. The doctrine of gender and age equality is applied to all its citizens.

Boys generally mature later than girls. By the time boys start to show physical signs of maturation most girls are well on their way to menstruation or have already passed this milestone. Eleven- to thirteen-year-old boys are well aware that the girls are changing fast and leaving them behind. It is an awkward time for sons and they often react defensively at this stage.

As boys transform psychologically and then physically, they spend much of their transition time in an exquisite state of internal tension and frustration. In Western culture this change is not acknowledged at all. Like girls, boys keep their sexual maturation a secret. The politically correct position is to ignore biological gender difference and change for the higher ideal of intellectual gender nondifference. For boys this means that validation of their maturation is actively sidestepped, even discouraged.

Mothers know when their sons start changing. A certain shyness and reluctance about childhood affections emerges as does secrecy about where he has been and what he has been doing. He has probably been hanging out with other boys doing deadly and dangerous things but he does not want his mother to find out. He seems to know that what challenges him or inspires fear will be obstructed or prevented by mother. Since she has the support of the law—which has been strengthened in all areas of sport, recreation, and leisure to minimize injuries—he surreptitiously creates and meets danger either on his own or with a group.

In groups boys cooperate in the development of an adventurous idea, give life to its shape, and design a strategy for its execution. Their world is one of action, of how to get from start to finish.

Mother remains the manager of all family activities and dynamics for as long as her offspring live at home. She is often reluctant or unable to embrace her son's maturation to manhood because her ability to control his movements and behaviors diminishes as his manhood emerges. In Western culture, mothers are supposed to control their sons until their education is complete, which is anywhere between the ages of eighteen and twenty-five.

During these years boys, like girls, attend compulsory, ideologically based school education. After school and weekends are their times for being boys, doing those things that emerging men choose to do. They invariably choose action and, where possible, physical action. This is their time to take risks, seek adventure, and confront death. Teenage boys can be found surfing waves or surfing the Internet, playing football, roller blading, and playing warriors and heroes in computer games about adventure. They are physically passionate and hungry for sexual experience and release. However, much of their innate sexual energy is dampened by a cloud of legal and social denial and oppression which has legislated away their opportunities for full-bodied physical expression. They must wear helmets, seat belts, and knee and shoulder pads and their games are regulated for safety with injuries of any sort condemned and outlawed. Older men guide younger men only in organized sports. In all other areas of their physical, spiritual, and emotional development adolescent boys rely on peers for direction because fathers, uncles, and significant older men are unavailable. There is no formal, structured rite of passage through manhood in Western culture.

And yet Western teenage boys and young men find their own ways to herald their physical and psychospiritual maturation. Sometimes the obligatory wounding happens through accident, competition, or high adventure. Sometimes in gangs or urban tribes they institute entry and progression standards, rigors, and markings. Tattoos sometimes appear on their upper arms or they wear rings in their ears or noses. Other tests of endurance, courage, or daring can mark their initiation. Sometimes they consume a killer level of alcohol on their twenty-first birthday. Sometimes their search for valid adventure is too difficult to find in the cushioned world of safety and motherhood so they break and enter houses, vandalize shopping centers, and steal cars. Police baiting has emerged as a popular and challenging pursuit for particularly disadvantaged adolescents who cannot drive legally, are far removed from access to public transportation, and have little disposable income. There are urban gangs of teenage and young adult males and the tribal warfare between them provides an outlet for the energies that their biology and physiology unleash.

Most teenage boys' journeys through adolescence to maturity are unmarked by rite, ritual, or incident. They tend to follow academic and training regimens whose focus is on employment in the workforce. There is no specific training for manhood, little guidance by older males, and no formal attention to any gender-specific powers, characteristics, or responsibilities. There is minimal training for relationship, marriage, or parenthood, and no sexual instruction from older men. What little training teenagers receive about these subjects is generally targeted at females, usually in the context of a class such as Early Childhood Studies. Teenage boys learn how to perform the sexual act through the popular media and their own haphazard experience, as do teenage girls. There is rarely any culturally contextualized learning offered about sex and sexuality, and nothing of its sacred place in relationship.

The profound transformation from boyhood to manhood and girlhood to womanhood slips by, acknowledged only by an academic tradition that expects that whatever happens physiologically and spiritually will inevitably be reflected in intellectual maturation, the only human development process endorsed by Western culture.

Jutta Malnic

Nagomorra site: sweetwater turtle dreaming.

Chapter Five

Coming of Age

Early Adulthood

She was a gorgeous, young white Australian artist who had been helping the old men record their sites. An excellent photographer, she captured images of the power in the land like no one else had. She projected slides of ancient rock paintings on the rich, red landscape and photographed the result. She brought the splendor of culture and country together for the world to see.

Away from her own culture and people for many months at a time, she became known to and desired by a young, full-blood Aboriginal man who pursued her silently for weeks but then could hold back no longer. He expressed his love for her, wanting to run away into the remote wilderness to set up camp.

The Lawmen found out and came to me saying, "You must talk to her. She cannot do this thing. He is in the Law and has a promise wife waiting for him. He must marry in the Wurnan system. He is wrong way for her. You Murranburra Lawwoman. You have to stop her from being sexy!"

To stop the matter from proceeding any further I asked the young woman to get on a plane or bus and come to Perth to sit with me on the verandah at Gidgegannup to talk things through.

She arrived the next day.

Why shouldn't she have a relationship with the young man? she wondered. We spoke of the differences in culture, the trust given to particular Whitefellas to work deep inside the Ngarinyin culture, trust given to honor and respect their Law. She recognized the level of protection given to her by the Lawpeople. The women had taught her how to fish, how to hunt for goanna and dig for yam. They trusted her with sacred knowledge. The old men gave her a skin group which made her taboo to all men of the tribe thereby protecting her from any ardent would-be lovers. Could she sacrifice all of that trust for the sake of an amorous liaison with a young man in the Law?

After a few days she wrote to the ardent young man to tell him they could only be friends because he has a promise wife already. She was very sad but knew her action was correct.

She had been waiting for this time since she was a young girl. She knew the man who was her promise husband because she had seen him regularly over the years as he brought gifts of kangaroo, emu, bush turkey, and ochres to her father's and mother's camp. But last rainy season, when his first wife died suddenly, he became ill himself so he surrendered his claim on her, passing the promise to his nephew whom he called brother. Although she had seen this young man a few times at ceremonies, they had never spoken because they were both in their taboo years.

For months since the knock-down rains heralded the bountiful, cool season, the young woman had been prepared for her marriage by the older women. It was now time to leave her family's camp to take her place with her promise husband and the women of his clan. She knew that this was the way it had happened for thousands of years, since time immemorial. It was her destiny.

The preparation for marriage had been completed by her aunt who, with other women of her family, laid her on a bed of leaves to open her up so that she would be ready for the act of consummation with her husband. In the cool of the night, away from camp, the older women, singing and cooing their task, gently caressed her, awakening her receptive power. Then they penetrated her womanhood to break the web that had protected her womb since she was born. They exhorted her, in their singing of the procreative songs of the Earth, to take on her responsibility and destiny as a woman in the fulfillment and embodiment of Wunggud.

In another world far away her promise husband had been prepared for marriage by older men of his tribe. His youthful, passionate, and explosive sexual urgency had now matured to a more patient, directed power, leavened with the consciousness of his responsibility and destiny as a man of the tribe in the power of Wunggud. He had been taught that he was responsible for the destination of his seed, that a prematurely conceived child would disrupt the pattern of life in Wurnan by being from the wrong skin group, clan, and land map. Such a child might be weak or damaged or might even die or be killed.

He had learned from the older men that the pleasure of sexual union is derived from joined bodies moving in concert with each other and the rhythm of life. They had shown him how to become rodlike, how to hold firm, and how to penetrate, move, and carry a woman to completion. Then he was sent to an older kinswoman of the tribe who taught him the skills of sex.

The overland journey to her promise husband was both long and enjoyable. The tribe moved through the land, walking from early morning, eating and resting in the hot part of the day, and then continuing the trek until Daughter Sun was low in the sky. They navigated by singing up the country.

A welcoming party was waiting a day's walk from the tribe's destination. They had been traveling for more than two weeks but their proximity to the promise husband's camp was foretold in dreams, and read in the smoke. Greetings were exchanged, sacred gifts given and received, and in the camp on that last traveling evening everyone participated in the songs and dance of the Earth in an exchange of goodwill and intent.

On arrival at the camp of her promise husband the young woman and her family were welcomed with the formal greetings of new relationships and the naming that confirmed the pattern of kinship as a reflection of the map of relationships in the land. Everyone greeted each other by their relationship name—mother-in-law, grandmother,

mother's sister's husband, father's brother's son, and so on. This naming of relationships is always necessary to commit and renew the land and people in the timeless Wurnan pattern of Creation which is maintained by the warp and weft of marriage, the human dimension of the eternally woven.

Prior to the marriage the couple are taken away for a week by an older relation of the promise husband. Here, in the privacy of their own camp, the couple learn how to look after each other's needs under the diligent guidance of their elder. They do not sleep together but become familiar with each other, learning the essential and intimate nature of each other's personalities and spirits. They hunt together, make camp together, and share stories, all the time privately noting and appreciating each other's strengths and skills. In the privacy of this isolation, they conduct themselves according to the rules of marriage and gender through which their roles and function have been defined under the watchful, helpful eye of their senior caretaker.

The marriage day arrives and the couple is returned to the camp where preparations have been completed by the men and women of the tribes. Food has been hunted, roots and nuts ground to powder ready for cooking in the coals as damper bread. Sugarbag is in plentiful supply, stored in bark bladders and hung in trees to keep the golden liquid fresh, cool, and safe from invasion by ants. Bush turkey, emu, and kangaroo have been killed, their intestines removed and cooked immediately to be eaten by the old men and women. The flesh cuts have been wrapped and stored in leaves, ready for the earthen firepits in which they will be slowly cooked.

The ceremony area has been swept clear of stones and sticks and a large circle marked out, at the center of which the firepit is marked by stones. Next to the pit is a pile of special leaves and a hair belt prepared by the women for the young couple.

When the marriage ceremony begins, all their kinsmen surround the couple in a large circle. Each group of tribesmen and women gather at the part of the circle that reflects the direction from which they traveled, the direction of their homeland. Within each tribal or clan group individuals sit in a pattern that reflects the relationship pattern within the group. All are joined in the circle and pattern of life which enfolds the couple standing in the center, protected and embraced by the power of unity within the living Wurnan.

The couple are entwined in the hair belt by a Lawman and Lawwoman. The fire, lit earlier and then subdued, is now fanned into life, a symbol of the new relationship. The man and woman, joined by their girdle of marriage, jump together over the brightly flaring fire. The leaves are placed over the flames and are immediately transformed into purifying smoke which engulfs the couple and spreads to all the participants in this sacred rite. Song, dance, and laughter now bubble forth as the couple, untouched by the others, is led away by two older kinsmen to their private camp.

Here a bed of leaves is prepared for the sexual consummation of their relationship. Under the protective shade of trees and the discreet, watchful eyes of their elders, the young man and woman lie with each other for the first time. They remain in this camp for several days with the old people who are available for any and all assistance in bringing about sexual comfort and compatibility. When the elders decide that the couple is ready to live as husband and wife, they all return to the main camp and the couple is embraced as fully married members of the tribe. Then they make their own camp within the pattern of the husband's tribe.

For the new young wife these weeks of preparation and her marriage into her husband's tribe herald the next stage of womanhood. She must bid farewell to her family who, with other witnesses to the ceremonies and rituals, will leave for their long return journey. She may not see her family until the next ceremony that brings the clans together to mark another rite of passage such as an initiation, or a marriage.

The older women of her husband's camp know the sorrow she experiences. They also left the camp of their fathers and mothers to take their place in another country, another clan. They know she will feel homesick for her family and familiar world and she will be shy as she learns her position and place in this new country with its different character, demands, and personality. They will have to guide her in the knowledge and skills that will serve and maintain her new clan. They will have to do this before she becomes pregnant so that she can raise her children in the Law and land of their father, their birthright country. The women understand that they must now assume responsibility for her as she becomes accustomed to her new role and functions as a wife. Her place in Women's Business will be fostered by them because she embodies and reflects the Law of her own country as all the wives do. The women are well aware that they are the embodiment of the design and integrity of the pattern of the land. The new wife's place in Women's Business will reflect this eternal pattern.

The women come from places throughout the region and their marriages into their husbands' clans constitute the completion of the Wurnan tapestry. The men remain geographically fixed as the warp of the pattern or map of land and Law while the women's movement from their own country into their husband's camp is the weft of the weave of Wurnan. When leaving their country, women do not surrender its Law. Neither do wives bring real estate into their husband's family's ownership or inheritance. Rather, they bring the Law, and responsibility for the land of their birthright country, into their husband's clan. This guarantees their Law and land's protection and stewardship. This pattern of land and Law is continually woven in the marriage system.

Once married, the new husband takes his rightful place in Men's Business as a full member of the community. Until his marriage he was excluded from active participation in decision making. The rite of marriage changed his status, and now, like the other older men of the clan and tribe, he must take responsibility for the care of his wife's land. Older men of the clan know they must guide him as he acquires the full knowledge of this new responsibility. He must learn the songs, dance, ritual, and ceremony of his wife's country so that when he takes her back to her birthplace, or joins other Lawmen in the rites and ceremony of initiation, or helps retouch the Wandjina paintings, he is able to sing up the country with them. He is now transformed from a single man to a married man with major responsibilities for land, Law, and his own progeny.

Perhaps because of its inauspicious history and its relative recency as a legally enshrined Christian value, marriage is possibly the most troubled of Western culture's institutions. The aspirations to high idealism espoused in the Christian Church's sacrament of holy matrimony is inherently compromised by its failure to address its origins in gender politics, and its contemporary social and economic implications. In the Western world today marriage is far more—and less—than the sacred union of man and woman. It is the dominant social and legal contract governing progeny and wealth.

The history of marriage is directly related to the history of land ownership. The modern Western world is built on the inheritance and ownership of land, and the power of capital to control the wealth it produces. For more than a thousand years the Christian Church has been so deeply involved in land acquisition and control that it has been heavily influential in shaping the pattern of land ownership and distribution of wealth throughout the Western world. With its roots in patriarchal values which inherently diminish and devalue the status of women, the church has historically been the chief culprit in dispossessing women of their birthright in both sacred and secular life. By wresting control of the rite of marriage from pagan and ancient common law the church institutionalized a woman's surrender of her land and wealth to the man, and subjugated her to her husband's authority in the marriage vows. This patriarchal Christian dogma was enshrined in English parliamentary law in 1753 and still lingers in some state legal statutes and the consciousness of men and women today.

In many Western countries early parliamentary laws have been amended to reflect the spirit of recent feminist objections, as have some Christian marriage liturgies; however, the roots remain as they were planted, and many modern laws and customs are still embedded in them. The primary influence of these roots continues to be evident in such customs as a woman changing her surname to that of her husband, the divorce settlement which values a breadwinner over a caregiver, common language usage that denies the independent value and contribution of a woman with references such as "John Stubbs and his wife," and formal greetings like "Mr. and Mrs. Edward Tinkerbottom."

While traditional religious marriage rites continue to be popular the trend in most Western countries is toward the secular ceremony. In recent decades, common-law or de facto marriages have become very popular in all age groups. While many young couples still opt for the full formal church wedding a significant percentage choose to simply live together because of the prohibitive cost of staging a traditional ceremony, or because they see little relevance in the religious rite. Many men and women whose first marriages fail are naturally more cautious about entering another binding contract, so they prefer to live in common-law relationships.

The modern laws that liberate a woman from being her husband's chattel simultaneously deprive him of the right to assume possession of his wife's wealth, or managerial responsibility of her estate. There is therefore less acquisitive compulsion for a man to marry now, while the maintenance of material independence is more important for many women. An increasing number of women today retain their birth names, maintain financial independence from their partners, and insist on individual ownership of all shared chattels. Because a majority of men and women now enter several marriages or monogamous relationships in their lives women often bear children from more than one father. Custody of children is therefore a major focus of postmarriage conflict, played out in the battleground of the secular legal system.

Some women, who are disillusioned with the whole idea of marriage or unable to find a suitable male relationship partner, or who prefer to be in a lesbian relationship, are now able to choose to be mothers without the involvement of a man at all. These women can be inseminated at a sperm bank and never know the identity of the father. The option of surrogacy is also available to women so that they can become biological mothers without themselves going through a pregnancy. In all these examples marriage, or even a relationship between a man and a woman, is unnecessary.

The traditional compelling reason for a man and a woman to enter the institution of marriage—the perpetuation of progeny and wealth—is now no longer relevant in most Western societies. While not all of the Western nations subscribe to such liberal thinking and practices, the trend has been set. Many Westerners, however, are disturbed by the possible consequences of this new liberalism, particularly the social instability that has emerged in their societies. In the push to release the religious shackles of marriage that once bound men and women in an unsatisfactory social, economic, and spiritual contract, indentity, intergenerational continuity, and community cohesion have diminished. That is not to say that there should be a return to the unsatisfactory but familiar ways of the early twentieth century, but in the cauldron of human consciousness there is an emerging awareness of the need for a living spiritual system to bind people together in shared values and rites. The fundamental relationship between man and woman and the spiritual union and public commitment to a shared identity are now being explored in many quarters within all Western societies.

Jutta Malnic

Mowaljarlai at Bush University, teaching about Wandjina
at Nagomorra site.

Chapter Six

Acquiring Wisdom

Maturity

The day was coming to its close, and the hunters were returning to the Marunbabidi camp with their catch. A group of elderly men sat around the firepit while the women sat further back, kneading damper dough. The young hunters joined the group, excited to tell of their adventure.

We were deeply involved in a discussion about Bush University, the Ngarinyin's cultural learning experience for Whitefellas. The young men waited patiently, eyes averted downward and away from the women's eyes. The women were Rambud, objects of mother-in-law taboo for these men, because they were the mothers of women who might become their brides so they had to avoid all direct contact, including conversation. We continued talking. A couple of young men sat down on the ground, and waited. Minutes later they were still waiting—listening patiently, but waiting. The conversation turned to how to involve young men in Bush University. Still they waited, saying nothing. After an hour passed, the young men wandered off without having spoken.

I said, "Why didn't we ask those young blokes what they would like to do for Bush University?" With what seemed to me to be gentle chastisement I was told, "They still young. They don't know anything yet. They still under our armpits. They got all their lives ahead of them. How can they know what to do in life while they still got all their living to do?!" The men and women all laughed loudly. What a joke! The trouble was, I didn't quite get it.

The warmth of the day is being sucked into the Earth, spinning into the vortex created by her molten core. Evening's chill falls rapidly with wafts of moist, cold air that make you shudder as they slide over your neck. More wood is laid on the campfire's edge so the coals that have been carefully nursed for cooking bread, goanna, and yams are not disturbed. In another part of camp, the Earth oven that holds the kangaroo has been stoked. Children dance their dares around the fiery circle and fling bits of twig, leaves, grasses, and food scraps into the flaring embers.

The kangaroo, yesterday's hunting prize, was prepared by the hunters. They burned off its hair and drained its blood into a bark and leaf container. They removed its internal organs and placed heated stones inside the carcass. Then the kangaroo was wrapped in leaves and lowered into a deep pit in which coals had been placed and covered with sand. Branches in full leaf were placed over the kangaroo, then more Earth. It has been cooking for nearly twenty-four hours. The evening before, the blood was heated and drunk like communion wine by particular men and women. The liver was removed by the hunters in the bush and cooked and eaten immediately. The kidneys and other intestines rich in protein, iron, and minerals were removed and cooked in the coals back at camp. These were then eaten by the toothless wise, elderly kin. The tasty, rich, fresh meat would be shared by everyone along with other food prepared by the women.

As the sun begins to set an old woman starts to sing, clapping a set of short sticks in a staccato rhythm. She sings the story of the setting sun, warning the children to observe and take it into their beings because Daughter Sun is very low in the sky now, marking the time when hunters, adventurous children, and all kinsfolk must hurry home. When the sun is in the fork of the tree, she implores everyone to hurry because she cannot hang on any longer. When she drops, it will suddenly be dark and dangerous.

Daughter Sun was sent to warm the Earth after her mother became too hot, and the people and animals, parched and dry from her scorching heat, begged her to send her daughter instead. When Daughter Sun emerged in the sky, she felt beautiful, and proudly rode across the arc of heaven. Snake, who thought he was the most beautiful creature in Creation, got so jealous that when Daughter Sun was directly overhead, he flew into the sky like a spear and bit her. Daughter Sun was badly wounded and, try as she might, she could not stay high in the sky. She kept sinking and sinking, wounded and in pain. As she slipped down toward the horizon, she started to bleed, and her blood ran right across the sky. Tired and weak, she hooked herself in the fork of a tree for a rest, trying hard to stay so that she could warm the world. Her efforts were in vain, however. She slipped out of the tree to sink behind the world. She told her mother the story of the jealous snake and her mother told her that after she rested and restored herself, Daughter Sun would be fine to go out across the sky tomorrow. Snake would be jealous of her and bite her so that again she would slip in the sky to return to her log behind the world and rest. That was her destiny.

The old woman sings about the Ri spirits of the ancestors, the mischievous Agula or devil spirits who lie in wait for those who leave their run home until it is too late. Hurry, hurry, she sings and taps.

The woman is too old now to go out on many hunting forays. She usually stays at the camp, either looking after children too young for the rigors of the day, or with other older men and women whose agility and endurance are insufficient for hunting. The old people laugh about their aging and physical limitations. One old man cracks a joke about some old fella who thought he was still a mighty hunter who could chase a goanna up a tree only to find that the goanna chased him up a tree from which he could not get down. His bones were just too old and stiff. Since that misadventure he had recognized that it was now time to concentrate on singing up the world, singing the totemic stories that renew the ties that bind all of Creation. He had made the passage into wisdom.

A few more older women join the solitary singer, adding their voices and sticks to the twilight celebration. Small children gather around, staying close to the warming fire while mothers prepare food for their families. Old men sit quietly by, humming in the Earth's resonance as a background for the women's songs. Not all the songs are teaching songs. Some are just plain funny, musical anecdotes sung to entertain the little ones. More people, young and old, join the groups around the fires. Care is taken to observe the Rambud mother-in-law taboo, and youth gender taboos that apply to adolescent boys and girls. This is achieved by making several fires so that people may share the evening's entertainment and laughter without breaking the taboo laws.

At another fire some distance from the main camp, a solitary old man hums to himself, seemingly oblivious to the activities of the two younger men who attend his every need. These two have been entrusted with the task of keeping the old man fed with a special diet of water, cool food, and no meat while maintaining a fire for his warmth. The old man—scarred, wizened, almost toothless—has been in humming bouts for several days, occasionally breaking into song but for the most part just swaying and humming. He is a Banman, a senior Lawman who through a regimen of extreme discipline, diet, and solitary ritual has attuned his mind and inner being to the voice of the cosmos, the song of the Earth, the messages of the ancestors. He must be served and protected from harm by his kinsmen in this altered state of consciousness for as long as it takes for the song to reveal itself through him to the tribe.

Banman is the frog, whose metamorphosis from egg to land-hopping, air-breathing creature embodies the raw elements of life—Earth, air, water, and fire. This Wunggud amphibian calls up the rains. He does this by spitting a fluid trail into the atmosphere which opens a gateway for Wandjina who in the form of lightning crackles his fiery response back to Earth. As Banman, the old man sends his psychic trail into the atmosphere opening a conduit for an inflow of cosmic knowledge in the form of sacred song. He must be well prepared for its power in body, mind, and spirit; otherwise it could kill him. His disciplined regimen for receiving the song lasts for weeks culminating in days of intensive self-preparation. The whole camp waits, always conscious that he is there getting ready.

As darkness falls, singing and dancing turns into performance and participation involving everyone in the camp. Stories from myth and from the day's adventures are reenacted. The old people tap and sing out the songs while children and their parents easily move into the patterns, persona, movements, and actions of the dance. At every day's end they dance and sing in a continuing celebration of their own embodiment and reflection of Creation. As the weight of darkness increases, the air begins to creep down people's bodies. Small children begin to tire and wander off into the laps of mothers and grannies. Soon everybody leaves for their camps. A man stokes up the fires for the night making sure no logs will fall, no flames or sparks will escape. He checks the surrounding area, noting the distant glimmer of light flickering through the bush from the Banman's camp. He senses that the old man will call everybody around him soon, perhaps tomorrow.

But it is several days before the familiar cry splits the air, summoning everyone to attention and attendance at the Banman's camp. The old man sits cross-legged on the ground, entranced. The song emerges from him. He waits as each phrase is repeated by everyone over and over and over until its very sound vibrates through the bones and flesh of every individual and the group. The song becomes a series of verses, each one describing an action until the sequence reaches its completion. Soon dance accompanies the song, and the Banman becomes each of the players in the action until others take up the parts. Sometimes the dance and song are for men only. Other times it is an open celebration for everyone's enjoyment. The Banman summons people on four consecutive days as he reveals to the tribe a full symphony. At the end of the song cycle, he collapses in utter exhaustion. For several weeks he is tended carefully by his appointed servers until he is able to return to the ordinary life of the camp.

Thus the song enters the knowledge and wisdom of the tribe. Sometimes the song is prophetic, sometimes it is a parable, but it always reflects the laws of nature. The song represents a revelation of Law for all the peoples in the land.

The old people in the camp are those whose teeth have begun to fall out. For women, this usually coincides with the cessation of their monthly menstrual cycle, and for men with the slow retraction of their testicles. Menopause often brings on the growth of whiskers in women, and testicular shrinkage is associated with the loss of body hair and enlargement of breasts in men. The bodies of both men and women change shape. They become more androgynous, physically, psychologically, and spiritually.

As they age, their eyesight also changes and they become more visionary or far-sighted with a simultaneous blurring of their near sight. This is the sign to the aging that they must leave the details of daily life to the clear-sighted, robust, younger men and women. The older people's vision now spans time and distance and since their focus is slow to change, they embrace change slowly. They take their time to allow their more mature breadth of vision to inform their decisions. They are secure in the knowledge that mind and body reflect each other in constant relationship, so that what happens to one is reflected in the other—physical and metaphysical. Their responsibilities change to reflect their altered eyesight and the assumed amplified insight that is embodied in the process of aging. These physical changes are considered signs of a maturing awareness, and are reflected in their roles and functions within the tribe. Whatever happens in the physical body becomes a symbol for their psychological and spiritual competence and awareness.

Having received the new song of Creation, the Banman returns to his kin's camp. There the old men sit together, exploring and absorbing its details and implications for the group. Younger men who are still in their hunting and breeding stage do not actively participate in these discussions. Their business is to maintain the physical health and well-being of the clan, and to protect all kin from all manner of danger, seen and unseen. They are sometimes allowed to listen quietly with their heads lowered respectfully. They do not, under any circumstances, interrupt the old men's conversation. Once when a young man rebelled at this respect by attempting to give his opinion about a matter under discussion, the old men simply stopped talking and sat in stony silence looking at a point in the Earth with unfocused eyes. They stayed in that position until, in a state of extreme physical discomfort, the young man left.

The old men's talk continues until a shared silence signals a general agreement. Before their agreement becomes a decision, however, they let a night pass. During the evening the old men take the issue and agreement to the older women, offering them a summary of their discussions. They then wait patiently until the women respond. This might be immediately, or in a few days' time, or not at all. There cannot be any action on decisions until there is a full women's and men's consensus. It is this way in the Law because everyone knows that, as in nature, everything returns to mother. It is mother who gives birth to the new, and warns the ignorant and unwary. Some discussions go on for whole seasons, even years, before consensus is reached. There is no sense of haste because the process of decision making is organic, not intellectually driven by time, goals, or strategy. Outcomes simply happen when it is their time.

The old women—Murranburra Lawwomen whose whiskers signify their maturity and wisdom—spend much of their time teaching younger women the healing and ceremonial arts. The Banman woman among them is the one who is able to heal by a laying on of hands, a particular mix of tinctures, and singing the powerful songs that invoke the healing Ri spirits. She knows about rubbing, touching, and heat healing methods. She has a full knowledge of local and exotic roots, leaves, bulbs, berries, and animal products, the whole natural pharmacopoeia. She often carries special stones and other sacred objects to release the Wunggud energy in both the agents of healing and her patients. She knows how to generate womb receptivity, control ovulation, bring on an abortion, and sterilize women who, for whatever reason, should have no more children. The Banman woman is feared and respected. She is always served by and deferred to by other women of the tribe and by all menfolk. In teaching young boys about the Banman woman, fathers and uncles warn them to fear woman because it is to her that they must return. Women, therefore, must always be respected and obeyed in matters of birth, survival, and relationship in both the physical and metaphysical domains. Old women's warnings are always heeded for fear of great retribution.

A frail old man, already thin, toothless, and in an almost continuous state of bliss, prepares himself for passing into death. A few years ago, he was captured by the Murranburra women and subjected to his last rite of passage. He, like his peers, knew that this rite was coming up, and together they conspired to protect each other from it. Old men know that when they pass through this last ritual, death, the final gateway to going home is imminent.

This last rite came about when the Murranburra women hijacked the old man when he was left alone at the camp one afternoon. They took him to their ceremony ground and laid him down on a bed of leaves. Holding his hands by his side, each of the Murranburra lowered herself onto his head and crawled astride him, rubbing her way down his body with her female parts. Completion of this ritual symbolizes his return to the womb of woman and indicates his readiness to return to the Earth from which he was born. From this rite until his death, he is able to participate fully in and discuss Women's Business for the first and only time in his life.

There is no such rite for women. Since they already embody the womb in their lives, they do not enact any ritual return. And since they give birth to males, they do not ritually enter Men's Business at any stage of their lives. They know that being female fully embraces the beginning *and* the end.

Ceremonial life in the land and within the tribe is maintained and taught by old men and women. They are the decision makers for all major actions, events, and ceremonies. Their special vision is respected without question because the whole tribe is trained to fulfill their biological potential at each age and stage. All stages are marked by physiological change and, in males, ritually consecrated in sacred ceremony. The status and respect embodied in being a Murranburra or Banman cannot be prematurely awarded. Being an elder comes exclusively with the physical changes that cause a person's vision to broaden, patience to expand, insight to grow, agility to weaken, and sexuality to androgynize. In other words, everything comes to the human in its time. In a culture where youth, cleverness, and physical prowess are valued for their usefulness to the integrity and viability of the tribe, these strengths never dominate. The elderly hold the Mythic intact, and through their achievement of the highest possible degree of cultural knowledge they remain essential to the survival of culture and heritage.

In Western culture, human value diminishes with age. The merit of experience has been replaced by qualifications, vision by expedience, and spirituality by wealth and power. Intergenerational cohesion and integrity have disappeared while guidance of the young by elders is but a memory from the predigital world. Youth are unsupervised and unguided because parents are too busy and afraid so they congregate in urban tribes or gangs far away from the influence of older people whose values they do not share, and who, in turn, show little interest in them. Aging is synonymous with redundancy. Once in their late fifties, men and women characteristically have little status, often struggle financially, have an ever-diminishing involvement in their children's families, and become increasingly invisible in worldly affairs. Many men die prematurely, often within months of leaving their workplace, while aging women constitute an increasing bulge in the population with an inevitable demand on health and medical services for diseases of the heart and spirit. This forgotten, invisible age and stage of life, from fifty-something to death, holds within it the history and memory of its society, culture, and wisdom.

An increasing number of men and women in Western culture are realizing an emptiness in their lives, particularly as they age. Many women seek divorce from their long-term partners and take up new careers in home-based self-employment that are often connected with the healing arts and human development. They do this in conjunction with other women either in collectives or in lesbian relationships. Many men are questioning the value of their work lives in terms of how they have improved society. In the final stage of their careers, many are taking forceful, radical positions in their search to leave a meaningful legacy for the next generation. By doing this they abandon the fiction of the importance of economic power and wealth in favor of a sustainable philosophy whose power lies in the generosity and integrity of the human spirit. There is a growing undercurrent of discontent with the direction of Western society and its current focus on material values. National strategies aimed at the maintenance and increase of economic growth rates are slowly losing their glamor as the rich get richer and the poor get poorer and wealth becomes increasingly concentrated in fewer and fewer hands. Men and women throughout the Western world are waking up for the first time in millennia to what has been lost, and to what is being rediscovered about Men's Business and Women's Business. They are exploring and encouraging a renaissance of old laws, the Earth laws of indigenous cultures which generate cohesive, spiritually based, integrated social systems. This new wisdom is coming from the very people who live in the culturally determined redundant stage of their lives.

My father worked in the insurance industry from the time he left school at sixteen years of age, when he started as a clerk at the bottom of the institutional ladder. For the next thirty years he worked his way up through the production arm of the organization. At the age of forty-five he changed from one company to another when he was appointed its production manager. By fifty he was being challenged by highly qualified actuaries who brought the new science of number crunching to the industry, and by fifty-five he was considered underqualified. With the continuing financial demands of his family he accepted a diminished job as branch manager of a regional office, where he was given the nickname "old man." At fifty-nine years of age he took early retirement, was given a gold watch at his farewell, and walked into his future seeing himself as a spent force.

After forty-three years of loyalty to just two institutions in the insurance industry my father entered his retirement a bewildered man who wondered what he was now good for. Until his retirement he justifiably prided himself on his excellent health and fitness and his active mind. Like so many other men in the same situation he became ill.

At the time I was working with traditional Aboriginal people in northern Australia in a job that required travel by four-wheel-drive vehicle through remote and hostile territory to the small, scattered Aboriginal settlements of Arnhem Land. My daughter was only two months old and was still being breast-fed. I was fortunate to be in a career where my clients considered motherhood an integral aspect of womanhood. My status was that of mature woman as I nursed my daughter while attending to business at hand.

On hearing about my father's illness and his loss of will to live I invited him to travel with me as my field assistant. This was not a bailout to save my father from premature death. I knew that to have an old man with me in my work would enhance my status even further because in Aboriginal culture the elderly command the authority and respect they deserve.

My father was no stranger to indigenous people because he was born in the Torres Strait Islands and grew up with the islanders. In many ways he was more comfortable with indigenous people than he was socializing with westerners. His contribution to my work was invaluable. Where I was excluded from participation in decision making because of my gender or age he was welcomed. He was privy to sensitive cultural knowledge reserved for old men, an experience that has made me wonder about the quality and integrity of information gathered by young men and women in pursuit of their master's and doctoral degrees that has since become historic or anthropological fact. My father always respected the privileged nature of the information the old men shared with him, but was able to guide and enrich my own assessments and understanding.

Here was a man who, having reached the age of sixty, was relegated to the margins of participation in his own culture while being held in esteem by Aboriginal people because of that same maturity. When he returned to his home in Melbourne he wrote of his experiences with the Aboriginal people of the Northern Territory. Later he went on his own to the Kimberley, where he spent considerable time traveling and talking with Mowaljarlai, his peer and friend. Both men, born within a few years of each other, had spent their adolescence in very similar mission settlements so they were able to bring valuable insight and a unique perspective to the early history of contact between black and white Australians. Much of Mowaljarlai's work with me has reflected their mutual sharing in a relationship that extended the unique interaction between our two families to four generations.

Christina Kennedy

Mowaljarlai showing Christina and Trevor Kennedy the Wandjina-like cartilage from the freshwater turtle at Bush University.

Chapter Seven

Journey to Dulugun

Death

We sat in the dining room enjoying morning tea. Most of the Whitefella workers met this way three times a day, then returned to their offices, stores, craft rooms, churches, and health centers. Forty of us lived and worked in the buildings of the central compound surrounded by more than six hundred traditional Aboriginal people from five tribal groups, each camp sited in the direction of their homeland.

The first scream cracked the air with its chilling message. A woman's full-bodied cry was soon joined by another, and another, the collective wailing penetrating ordinary sensibilities like shards of glass. Too soon, a messenger arrived to tell us that there had been a fight. A young man's skull had been cracked open by a drunken kinsman wielding a wooden club called a nulla nulla. Still just alive, the young man was removed from the camp and carried to a clinic.

As morning turned to midday, the crowd of women and men seated in the dirt around the clinic's verandah steps grew as did the intensity of their crying. We were all put on notice. If the man died, we were to take extra care in our movements and security because the incident could provoke a bout of "get-back," an avenging violence *that, if exacerbated by alcohol, could become very serious. The clinic had already issued an urgent call to the Royal Flying Doctor Service, and was working furiously to sustain the victim's vital signs. At lunchtime the distant drone of the air ambulance was detected on a puff of wind. Relief swept through the mission compound. The man was safely evacuated, his hold on life extremely tenuous.*

At midafternoon another urgent call split the airwaves, this time for the Halls Creek police to come and get the perpetrator or he would surely be injured or killed. The family of the drunk young man begged the priest/superintendent to get him out and locked up for his own safety. Another, lighter plane was soon heard coming from the north, and a familiar blue and white aircraft arrived. The police quickly took the offender on board and left.

Now it was just a matter of time. The whole settlement waited in suspense for news of the victim. Three days later, we were notified that the man was going to live. Eight months later, just after his release from jail, the perpetrator was carried to the clinic with severe spear wounds in his legs.

A single, unmistakable, spine-tingling wail split open the dawn. An old man had gone home, had started his death journey to Dulugun. His young wife's wail was soon joined by the wailing of more women and men. Children watched, big eyes even bigger because of the new day's unfolding drama. They were unsettled even though they knew the inevitable course of events that would dominate their lives for the next week. They knew about the young mother whose baby died at birth. She still carried her dead child, tightly wrapped in bark, until she knew it was time to place the little bundle in a rock hollow in the Wunggud place of its origins.

With its maddening, mind-penetrating force, the wailing grew in pitch and crescendo until the birds stopped flying. Stones were used by the wailers to crack themselves on their heads until blood poured to the Earth. Nothing else was audible in the world—only this forceful outpouring, this expression of grief in tears and blood.

The wailing and self-wounding went on into the day as more people joined the death rite. A group of older men, led by a Banman, walked to a sacred Men's Business area where they began to construct a death platform on which they would lay their kinsman. Chanting as they worked, they cut young trees and fashioned them into a frame supported at its ends by the forks of two living trees. When complete, the platform stood chest-high. They worked energetically and mindfully because they knew the spirit of the dead man was still in and around the camp. They had to be sure he did not become upset, and that their preparation for his passage between the worlds was correctly done. Their singing reflected the knowledge that they had several simultaneous spirit manifestations of the deceased to respect, each in its own way.

There is a song that carries the man's Gi to his Earthly place of rest in the Wunggud of his origins. His Gi is the totemic energy spirit that gave him identity and relationship with the Earth, and his place in the Wurnan. His incarnate, totemic spirit will rest in a Wunggud waterhole until it is born again in another child. Many of the children in the camp are infused with such spirits, embodying the identity and Gi of ancestors. One old man tells the story of his wife calling out "Emu, emu!" Later, on a hunting trip, that man shot an emu through the chest. The spirit of that Wunggud emu, a relation who had died earlier, became their son who was born with a scar on his rib cage exactly where his father had shot him when he was an emu. Other children come from spirits of the Milky Way, or ancestral spirits.

Then there is a song that prepares to open the gate to Dulugun, the land of the spirits in the islands offshore where all deceased people go and live forever as teachers of the Banman, the source of sacred song. The sun does not shine in Dulugun yet there is no darkness. A dead moon shines with a soft perpetual light like an eternal dusky sunset. In Dulugun there is plenty of food and eternal happiness, a deeply primordial place where the marshes are boggy, and the slime stinks like flying fox. It is a rain forest and mucky underroot place where hard land is scarce. Dulugun is only seen by those Banman who travel the death cord in a trance and return with a song. Even the food in Dulugun is smelly and unpalatable to mortals.

The pathway to Dulugun is dangerous so great care must be taken in opening this gateway. People have been caught in the energy of Dulugun's golden thread or death cord, and disappeared only to return as ancestral spirits. If anyone mucks around while the gateway is open, they can get sucked into the chasm that transports people between the worlds. If this happens, there is no way of returning unless they are protected and held in this world by the Banman and other men who sing the correct sacred song to anchor themselves in the energy of the cord and in the chasm to fly the lost ones back.

Ancestral spirits are ever present and must be properly honored at all times. Sometimes, when the west wind blows, ancestral spirits leave Dulugun when it is neither night nor day but twilight, the intersection of time and space when Earth and heavens mingle in reflections of each other. The spirits travel in the lightstream of the energetic cord between the worlds, and roam around in their Wunggud places among the living. They are often seen, and are frequently involved in active communication in song, dance, vision, and dream.

After the body is placed on the death platform, the older men carefully surround the platform with stones and the mourning continues. Before sunset, all the man's material possessions were collected and smoked. The tribe must protect the dead man's spirit from being trapped in his possessions, and smoking them releases his spirit on its transformational journey to beyond this world and ensures that his spirit is not held back. This allows the spirit of the dead man to stay to guard its body until all the flesh has dropped off it. His name will not be spoken by anyone. In fact, nobody will use his name for several years for fear of bringing his spirit back, or locking his spirit in the person who said his name. If another person has the same name, its use is dropped, and another totemic name is activated.

The stones that are brought by the men are the tools used to make an inquest into the death. This is more significant when the deceased has died prematurely. The kidney fat of the deceased will drip onto a particular stone to uncover the identity of a murderer if there is one. If identified, the murderer would learn of the result from a Lawman, or by recognizing that he had been sung. His own death would soon follow. In the case of this old man, however, the inquest stones are used symbolically because the man died of old age.

A year, sometimes two years later, when all the flesh is gone from the skeleton, the elders return to prepare the old man's bones and spirit for the next stage of the death rite. They remove him from the platform, and proceed to clean his bones, washing them until they are pure white. The men then anoint the bones with kangaroo fat to strengthen his spirit with the spirit of the animal, a repeat of the rite he underwent at his initiation time. The bones are then rubbed with red ochre, the incarnation of kangaroo blood, to acknowledge that the man's being is multidimensional, made of physical, ancestral, and mythic spirits. The men then carefully place the bones inside a paperbark wallet, ready for the great mourning ceremony that is still to take place when the whole community of kinsmen initiate the old man in the next stage of his journey, his spiritual return to the living.

Just before sunset that evening, the mourning ceremony starts when the old man's kinsmen, painted in the ochre symbols for this rite of passage, sit wailing around the wallet holding his anointed, now untouchable bones. Again, women and men strike themselves on the head with axes, clubs, or stones to grieve the absence of his spirit and to call it back from death's darkness into the light of the living. He has been in the darkness since he died and now they want his spirit to walk with them in the camp, to be among his kinsmen.

The Banman and the Murranburra men set up two poles close by, between which is a tightly stretched cord of human hair. This represents the death cord that marks the boundary between life and death, light and darkness. All the kinsfolk wait on the light side—or sunrise side—of the cord. Only the Banman can withstand the forces of darkness on the death side, the sunset side. He must pass the wallet coffin across the cord into the light in order to allow the dead man's spirit to live again. At dusk, the Murranburra men, led by the Banman, sing and dance the ancestral spirits into participation. Just before the sun slips over the world, they pass the wallet of the dead man from the empty darkness of death across the cord into the spirit of light in the community, at the same time cutting the cord. The timing of this step is crucial because the movement of spirits can happen only in this moment. There is much rejoicing when the passage is complete.

From the time of death to this moment, the man's widows have been isolated from the rest of their kinsmen. Soon after he died, all the women whose birthright made them promise wives to the man in his lifetime cut off their hair and assumed widow behavior. They retreated into a life separate from their kinsmen, a sign of mourning and respect. All their possessions—their baskets, tools, traps, sleeping mats, and clothing—had been collected, smoked, and redistributed to other women who were not wives. During this time of isolation, they are served and looked after by their families, and have been resupplied with gifts of new tools and clothing from other women. But they have not participated in any group hunting or gathering, nor eaten meals with their kinsmen. They are taboo in all respects until the mourning time has passed and the man's bones returned to the community. This rite signifies their release from the taboo and from their widow behavior, and they are reunited with their families at this joyous time.

A "mother" of the dead man—either his biological mother, a sister of hers, or another close kinswoman—receives the wallet coffin, welcoming him home. She will look after it until a full year's cycle of change has passed. Now that his spirit has come alive and rejoined the community to camp with them all, everyone is happy. All of his kin will spend some time with the wallet of bones, welcoming his spirit to their presence. As they adjust in their roles, relationships, and responsibilities, he is there as participant. He is cared for constantly in death as in life. During this time, the gap that his physical death left in the Wurnan is carefully rewoven to maintain the integrity of the kinship system as reflected in the land. Death is, after all, a disturbance in the physical pattern of life, the action of Creation, so it must be organically and mythically absorbed and integrated.

As the seasons change, the Murranburra men know that the dead man's spirit wants to leave the living, and go home to rest in his own Wunggud place. He has been locked up in the paperbark wallet for a complete cycle of seasons. Now he wants to go home to the Wandjina in whose image he was created. The Murranburra men take the wallet from the dead man's kinswoman and leave. They may be away for several weeks because the man's Wunggud place is in the stony country where the great rivers were carved out by the Wunggud Snake. As they walk, the men sing up the country, knowing that as the song emerges in their consciousness so the country's features and spirits will emerge. Every song and each verse comes from that interior place within them that is attuned to the Earth, her shape, and her Creation. As long as they stay attuned to their relationship with the Earth, and sing up her vibrations, they will stay on course.

When they reach the Wunggud place, they climb to the cave where the bones of those who have gone before are laid out to rest. The cave is a wide slit in the rock face, invisible from the ground. An overhang protects the bones from exposure to rains and wind. Below the shelter are massive rock formations, sacred and powerful. Wandjina imprinted himself in these rocks, telling the story of Creation in this place. The dead man was created by this Wandjina and here the Murranburra open up the wallet to set the man's spirit free. He can come and go as he likes now, happy to be integrated into the Creation place from which he originally emerged. The Murranburra make a bark bucket which they fill with water from the dead man's Wunggud, the sacred waters from which his life came. They place this beside the opened wallet.

The Murranburra men are very happy to have returned their kinsman. They know that once he is released from the wallet coffin, his spirit will return to its Wunggud in the water and make its final journey to Dulugun. Once there, he may return as Agula, the trickster who comes on the west wind to walk among the living. But first he must travel through the gateway to the land where the sun does not shine, where the dead moon glows his subdued light, and the waterfalls gurgle.

As they return to their kinsfolk's camp, again singing up the country to guide their journey, the Murranburra men stop to hunt, and make a traveling camp. Here they sing into the night. One Murranburra recalls his experiences of visiting Dulugun. The other talks easily of his meeting Agula in the spirit of a man long deceased, on a hunting trip in the dead man's country. His bones were in a resting place close to where the hunter made his camp. The hunter's son was born in the spirit of this deceased and was a reincarnation of that ancestor. The hunter had also seen the dead man's spirit when he journeyed through the chasm on the cord to Dulugun. This spirit was simultaneously present in Creation as the hunter's son, in the sacred Wunggud water of the deceased's origin, in his whip snake totem, as Agula the trickster spirit from Dulugun, and in the Milky Way where all the ancestors live after they journey to Dulugun. Unconfined and undefined by time, space, dimensions, realms, or perceptions, the spirit of the dead man lives in all aspects of Creation's idea and action, wherever his existence named him. As a prism simultaneously reflects light in many directions, so the spirit of the dead reflects images in all the realms of experience.

While everyone knows that death comes to us all, westerners have such a generalized fear of it that governments and private institutes finance scientists to spend years trying to find new ways to prolong life. This field of medical research is not confined to the development of new drugs and treatments for those whose young lives are afflicted by disabling conditions and terminal illness, nor to the prevention and cure of pandemic diseases such as AIDS and influenza that claim too many lives. Much of its focus is to explore ways to arrest the natural process of aging and to extend the lives of the elderly beyond the collapse of their vital organs and altered minds. Westerners are generally not comfortable with death and dying, and prefer to avoid embracing the process of a life's ending with the same rigor that is applied to birth and all other passages of life.

The preservation of human life has become a creed of such magnitude that a single life and death issue can influence the outcome of a national election. In the last thirty years the extension of fundamental human rights to include the right to choose to die has been a focus of political, religious, and social debate in every democracy of the Western world. The life and death debate extends to abortion, euthanasia, cryogenics, cloning, and the use of life support systems to keep human beings alive when all vital signs have left them. The yearning for immortality seems to have become a scientific and cultural obsession.

Not all Western nations pursue death avoidance with such vigor. Countries that embrace formal religions whose credos promise life beyond the grave are less concerned with the postponement of death. The main impetus for death defiance comes from wealthier nations whose living myth has changed from the spiritual to the material. While wealth and materialism can control or modify almost every other passage of human existence, it cannot stop the inevitable ending of life. Death confronts the materialist creed, the fallibility of which is exposed in its failure to sustain life indefinitely. It opens up the deepest vulnerability of the human spirit, to which the creed of materialism brings little comfort or meaning.

Loved ones often report that a dying relation has disclosed a spiritual experience in which their whole life was played back to them like a video on fast rewind. At the end of the experience the person laughed with the realization that the lifelong pursuit of possessions was to no avail. Nothing can be taken beyond the grave. Everyone leaves the world as they enter it. Many regret squandering opportunities to nurture relationships, or spending too much time at the office or in careers that took them away from family life. Many search for meaning or God as their life force weakens and fear sets in. Many report that for the first time they feel released and relief that it is all over now. At last they feel a quality of peace that had eluded them in their lives as they pursued happiness through material goals. For many of those left behind, the grief they feel is not only for the loss of the significant person, but for the loss of those opportunities to realize the promise of loving relationships and spiritual sharing.

In most Western societies funerary rites are generally based on Christian practices that espouse burial or cremation. However, the rite itself can be secular, conducted by a civil celebrant. While paid specialists organize the logistics of a funeral, the procedures and program are usually discussed with the close family of the deceased. The family's responsibility is to provide clothing for the body, select a casket, make decisions about whether there will be a viewing and who will be permitted to attend, nominate pallbearers, choose the chapel flowers, notify newspapers, send out invitations, and organize a reception after the funeral.

The method of disposal of the body is regulated by the state. Burial in the ground is usually confined to designated areas such as cemeteries or churchyards. Burial at sea must comply with regulations. Disposal of ashes is probably the most flexible option. Preparation of the body is conducted by the undertaker who, in the case of a body that is to be laid out for public viewing, applies special makeup to the head, neck, and hands.

The funeral rite can be a very expensive exercise because many westerners want to honor and reflect the deceased's worth and stature in society. This is usually expressed in the size and complexity of the service, the decoration of the casket and chapel, and the pageantry of the funeral procession. In other countries the adornment of the casket and tombstone are intended to reflect the deceased's place of importance with the extended family and act as an offering to God in the belief that His protection will abound if generosity and filigree have been demonstrated in temporal life.

In some Western societies grief is considered a private matter so public displays of emotion are considered weak or indelicate. In others the public outpouring of emotion is considered an indication of the depth of the person's feeling and loss. In recognition of the long process of grief and the difficulties that can emerge when death is not fully embraced, grief counseling and support groups are available in most Western societies. This trend is evident in countries where the political agenda encourages freedom of religious expression and the population has become separated from the traditions of a formal state religion and the rites and ceremonies that accompany spiritual passages in life and death.

As the final rite of passage, death is possibly the most perplexing in Western culture. The central question in many people's minds is what happens after the life force leaves the body. They wonder if there is life after death, if the soul is a reality or a myth, if the loved one might return reincarnated in a recognizable form, or if death is final for body, mind, and spirit. Many who have had near-death experiences talk about the bright light and the tunnel, the review of their lives, the choice to return to their bodies and the transformation that they experience as a result. Where there is no shared religious system or spiritual beliefs the questions often remain shrouded in fear. It is natural to fear the unknown, but when fear is experienced as terror the fight for immortality surfaces. This seems to be a significant trend in much of the Western world.

Once, while David Mowaljarlai was staying at my Gidgegannup farm, he was told of the death of a Whitefella project officer who had worked with him in Derby and had since been working with Aboriginal people in Halls Creek in the East Kimberley. The man was only forty-something and suffered a heart attack while driving to an outlying community. His family lived in Adelaide, so his body had been flown there for the identification and the funeral service. A teenage son who had visited him often in the Kimberley and had recently been living with him in Halls Creek convinced his family that his father would like to be buried in the lands of the people with whom he had spent his life working. A compromise was reached. The man would be cremated in Adelaide and his ashes returned to the Kimberley for dispersal.

The young man and his uncle, accompanied by a group of adopted Aboriginal relations, arrived at Gidgegannup to discuss this possibility with Mowaljarlai. Never before had a Whitefella's remains been handed over to Aboriginal people for their ceremonial disposal. Mowaljarlai was entirely agreeable; the man had been a good friend, and Mowaljarlai had watched the son grow from boyhood.

When they left, Mowaljarlai voiced his fears and doubts, wondering how his Ngarinyin, Worrora, and Wanumbal relations would deal with the proposition of opening up the death ceremony to a Whitefella. He did not know how cremation worked, and wondered how big the urn containing the ashes would be. I told him that the body goes into a big oven where it is burned up with intense heat, and then the bones are crushed up to a fine powder and placed in a vessel about as big as his hand. He was amazed that a big man's body could be reduced to a handful of ashes. He wondered how cremation fit in to the Ngarinyin rite and at what stage in the journey to Dulugun the man might be. He wanted to know what Whitefellas did with the ashes. I told him that they could be placed behind a brick in a cemetery building, buried under a rosebush in a crematorium garden, or scattered in a place that was special to the deceased.

Mowaljarlai returned to Derby to talk with his kin. Three weeks later the man's brother and son traveled to the Kimberley ready for the adapted Ngarinyin rite. A large group of Aboriginal men and women from several communities met at a remote waterhole half a day's drive from the nearest settlement, where Mowaljarlai arrived with the urn of ashes. The Lawmen painted themselves in totemic symbols, then sang up Creation as they do in their traditional ceremony, calling in the spirits of the animals, birds, and lizards to witness the passage to Dulugun of this Whitefella friend. After sunset and many hours of singing and dancing the songs of the country a group of senior men, accompanied by the man's uncle and son, took the ashes further along the Wunggud waterhole to the spirit place where they were ceremonially dispersed across the waters. Then they returned for the feast of bullock, yams, and damper bread that the women had prepared.

The next evening as Mowaljarlai and I had a cup of tea at my motel in Derby he told me that when he was a young man he was sent away for training to become a Christian minister. He had learned the Scriptures, the Christian rites, and how to run a ministry. When he was fully prepared for induction he was told that the time was not right, that as yet the church was not ordaining Aboriginal people into a full ministry. Instead he could assist an ordained Whitefella in a town or mission settlement ministry, and could serve God and His people as a special church elder. For forty years Mowaljarlai had wondered why it was that Aboriginal people who were trained in exactly the same way as Whitefellas could not be ordained. But that didn't matter here. As he got up to leave he said, "Anyway, we did a good job for that poor Whitefella, didn't we?"

Christina Kennedy

Two-Way Thinking in action: Jillian Bangmorra and Hannah Rachel Bell teaching Women's Business beside the Marunbabidi Wunggud waterhole at Bush University.

Chapter Eight

Two-Way Thinking

When I was first introduced to Men's Business, Women's Business, I thought it was a quaint but outdated code of conduct for human behavior. After all, hadn't women spent decades breaking down this "artificial" definition of gender which had for so long rendered females second-class citizens? Weren't women just as capable as men of doing absolutely anything at all? I was enthusiastic to learn about Men's Business, Women's Business because I wanted to "help the Aborigines" move into the twenty-first century as fully potentialized, aware humans just like westerners. I could do this only if I understood the way they conducted their lives in the present. I was very young, still in my twenties.

As the years passed, I discovered a fantastic depth, consistency, and wisdom in this ancient knowledge and its behavioral protocol. Men's Business, Women's Business is far more than simply a code of conduct for men and women designed for social cohesion; it is a true reflection of the Law that ultimately governs the behavior of everything. The Law is that there are *always* two, and these are *always* in dynamic, interactive relationship. Men's Business, Women's Business is this Law's human face.

The Ngarinyin marriage system is based on a sophisticated understanding of this Law. According to the Ngarinyin, everything "standing up alive" is born as either Wodoi or Djingun. These moieties embody the masculine principle and the feminine principle respectively. In humans, moiety is passed through the father while the Law is carried by the mother. Women leave their own clan to live with their husband's clan, carrying their own Law with them. Their husbands must honor and protect this Law. Men marry not only women from the other moiety, they also marry her land which they then must serve and protect as a man serves and protects his wife. The marriage system goes even further in that not every woman of an opposite moiety is necessarily an eligible, or promise wife. She must also be named by, and belong to, a specific geographic locality which has its own characteristic land, flora, fauna, and water types. Their marriage system is a human map that reflects the land and its ecology. Consequently a stony-ground woman might marry a sandy-ground man, or a saltwater man might marry a freshwater woman. The pool of "right way" women for men is both self-defining and self-limiting.

Mowaljarlai explained this system to me over many years. As he gave examples, I plotted the story in diagrams. It came as a great surprise to find that my diagram for the Ngarinyin marriage system looked exactly like a model of the DNA molecule. As this story unfolded, I found that the relationships between and functions of genes on chromosomes correlated with the functions prescribed for males and females in Men's Business, Women's Business, including the Ngarinyin rites of passage!

When we explored the biologically determined ages and stages of human male and female maturation with their characteristic changes in physical and mental capabilities, Mowaljarlai would tell a Ngarinyin story that both describes and guides this metamorphosis. Frogs, for example, go through not just the three characteristic stages of metamorphosis identified in the Western paradigm but three additional ones. The extra stages in Ngarinyin knowledge relate to not only the appearance of the changing amphibian but to its capabilities and behaviors. Each of these stages correlates with identifiable, gender-specific passages in human maturation. This whole story is captured and celebrated in a single, sacred painting hidden in a rock shelter in

Ngarinyin country. Likewise the process of growth of a tree from a tiny seed to a fully mature specimen is identified according to the behavioral characteristics of each stage. These stages are analogous to the stages of the male and female frog and human. In the Ngarinyin culture, every example of visible life is celebrated in stories and songs that tell of its origins, cycle, and death, as well as in rock paintings and engravings.

Once while driving through Ngarinyin plateau country with a small group of visitors attending Bush University, I was explaining how the Ngarinyin view of the landscape was different from the way westerners view the scene, introducing the visitors to the mythic view of the world, where the actions of nature, humans past and present, and ancestral spirits are inseparable. Whereas Europeans see ant mounds, trees, or a geological formation as separate from each other, the Ngarinyin see stories of Creation in which they are integral characters. At this point Mowaljarlai said, "See those trees? They are all hip to hip together. They are dancing their story. Swinging and swaying in the wind. We call that Yorro Yorro. Everything standing up alive. And that escarpment there? That's the story of the yam. The little boy was running along there, crying. The water from his nose dripped into the ground. Those places are yam places. All those trees, all those yams, that escarpment, they're all tied together by energy cords. The spaces between them are light energy. The trees and rocks are like electricity poles, transmitting the energy that runs through all of Creation, keeping everything in its place."

Months later I was sitting on my verandah watching the wind blow through the reeds in a lagoon. I noticed the reeds moving in waves in what seemed like a dance. I had been reading a popular book on quantum physics, trying to come to grips with the difference between wave theory and particle theory. Looking at the reeds, I was struck with the thought that this was wave theory in action. The relationship between the wind and the reeds was a bit like cracking a whip in slow motion, sending waves down its length and back to their point of origin. As I focused my attention on the tips of the reeds, I noticed that there was a little popping sound as the wind cracked the reeds like a whip. While focused on the crackling tips, I could no longer see the wave motion. This was particle theory in action. Then I became aware of something in myself. While I was looking at the tips, that was all I saw. While looking at waves, I did not, could not, see the tips. In other words, I saw what I was looking for. I was very excited by this observation because suddenly I felt I was starting to see what Mowaljarlai had described in the Kimberley—trees united by energy cords dancing hip to hip. This way of seeing has never left me. Now it is only when I consciously focus on a particular item in a view that I stop experiencing the totality of life's dance.

One of the distinguished visitors to Ngarinyin Bush University was the Right Reverend Dr. Peter Carnley, Anglican archbishop of Perth, whose visit was the subject of an Australian Broadcasting Corporation documentary film for their *Compass* program. After a week's saturation in Ngarinyin philosophy, beliefs, visits to rock art sites, and participation in secret Men's Business and sacred ceremony, he stated that prior to Bush University he thought that Aboriginal spirituality was probably rooted in a kind of pantheistic mythology and doctrine. He now recognized that their spiritual practice was far more complex and inspiring. He called it "pan*en*theistic." He said this was different from pantheism, a doctrine that identifies the deity with the universe. Here was a philosophy in which the Divine is the source *and* the spirit of Creation with an added dimension of "beyond our understanding." What Mowaljarlai described as the energy cord that unites everything is also the energy supply that enlivens everything, and gives Creation its texture and shape. This is Wunggud, the blueprint of Creation. It manifests first as an idea. Then, with the energy of its own intent, it projects the idea into a physical form. Through this means Wunggud imprints itself on rock walls in the form of a painting. It is the glue of Creation as well as the resonance, the life force. The nature and essence of Wunggud that is comprehensible is always manifest in *relationship*, the primary, universal, governing law of nature.

The rock art tradition of this part of the Kimberley region is world famous. It can be found only in the homelands of the Worrora, Wanumbal, and Ngarinyin, the three tribes whose destinies are absolutely and irrevocably linked in the Wurnan system. This art is found in rock shelters of the seven river systems, their gorges, and waterholes. There are literally hundreds of galleries containing these paintings, the Wunggud's communiqués with the tribes. In many galleries, the paintings span more than thirty thousand years of human history right up through today. This is the story of the evolution of human consciousness. Wandjina, the most recent of the many art forms, is still the oldest single icon to be repeated throughout a distinct region, and is apparently the earliest expression of monotheism on Earth. While Wandjina is usually male, it is sometimes female.

According to the Ngarinyin, Wandjina is Wunggud's agent or messenger. They assert that no human designed any of the art forms, including the Wandjina image. Instead Wunggud, in the spirit of Wandjina, vibrated the images from inside the rock to its surface. Then the designated Lawmen, in a state of ecstatic attunement, follow the outlines and specific colors to create the paintings. In this way Wandjina causes the paintings to become imprinted in rock shelters as Wunggud's communiqués with the tribes. In Ngarinyin tradition, the appearance of the different images follows a sequence that accords with the Western archeological view. The first paintings were of hunted animals and gathered berries and plants. Then came the Guyon Guyon paintings, sometimes ignorantly called Bradshaws after their European discoverer. These exquisite humanlike figures, with their once colorful and decorative body adornments, represent the gift of ceremony and ritual. They also communicate the gift of stone tools and technology to the tribes. Where a number of figures line up with hands outreached to each other, they represent the sharing system between tribes. The Earth Mother and mother come next, represented by a Wandjina-type female figure in the act of giving birth and calling on the tribes to respect her. Wodoi and Djingun appear as two types of owls, and with them comes the story of how these two kinship laws came into being. The owl is a sacred bird because it sees all in the darkness of the human dreaming state. Wunggud's gift of moral law comes in the Dumby story. Finally came the Wandjina tradition and with it the gift of love. When all of Creation had been communicated, Wandjina imprinted himself on the wall, often overlaying all preceding communiqués, as the incarnation of Wunggud.

It is Wandjina that is kept alive by the tradition of ceremonially retouching the paintings, a task that is undertaken by special Banman men. Wandjina is kept freshly painted to ensure that the rains for which he is responsible are replenishing and renewing rather than destructive. Wandjina is always found near waterholes. As the sender of rain, he empties himself into the indentations created by the Wunggud Snake when she coiled up to rest during her Creation journey through the land. Wandjina, the incarnate messenger of Wunggud, and Wunggud Snake, creator of the means of gestation and birth, represent the now familiar relationship of male and female. Water itself is male when it is sent in storms, cyclones, and rain clouds but it becomes female when it rests quietly in the Earth as a waterhole, the medium through which life comes into being.

Wandjina has fascinated archeologists and rock art specialists since the paintings were discovered by westerners at the turn of the twentieth century. Described variously as aliens, a cult hero, or gods, Wandjina is the only rock art in the world where the peoples to whose tradition it belongs continue to interact with it in the exercise of retouching.

During one of Mowaljarlai's and my marathon discussions, the mystery of Wandjina began to unravel. Mowaljarlai was explaining the relationship system to me. I always find it helpful to create a graphic, a kind of diagram that reflects the shape of the information I am trying to absorb. As he talked about Wodoi and Djingun, marriage, relations between individuals, couples, clans, Men's Business and Women's Business, man and land, and so on, I found that the graphic emerging on my paper was a picture of Wandjina. The circles and dots represented female place and function while the lines and dashes represented male place and function. Wandjina, as well as being the incarnation of Wunggud, could be seen as a single graphic formula for the Law of Relationship.

The most often asked question about the Wandjina is why there is no mouth. Mowaljarlai explained that the void is unspeakable because it is beyond our understanding. Years later, as I tried to come to terms with computer technology, I learned that it all operates on patterns of 0 and 1. It was amazing to me that the ancient Wandjina and twentieth-century technology used the same two symbols to create patterns for communication with the world.

The utter consistency of the basic premise of Ngarinyin philosophy throughout every facet of cultural and social life defies explanation. After more than two decades of listening, challenging, and learning, I continue to discover the contemporary relevance of their stories and way of seeing. In 1989 Mowaljarlai and I decided to name the Ngarinyin worldview "Pattern Thinking" because the whole of their cosmology is inextricably interconnected according to, and as a reflection of, the immutable Law of Relationship. By comparison, the Western way of seeing is reductionist, linear, singular, and fragmented while its law is made by men with power and is very changeable. We named this system "Triangle Thinking" because power concentrates in an ascending cone toward the top where One rules. Pattern Thinking reflects the Law of Relationship, so not only are there no bosses but relationships are an integrated pattern between the masculine and the feminine. Triangle Thinking, the system of relationships for all patriarchal civilizations, reflects the power of the masculine One and its authority to own, control, and hold dominion over all else. Pattern Thinking and Triangle Thinking seem, at first glance, mutually exclusive. The fact is, however, that as we approach the third millennium, both are unsustainable in their own right, and both have much to learn and incorporate from each other. Pattern Thinking in its original form is unsustainable because of the very Law of which it is a reflection. Because Ngarinyin Law is a reflection of the laws of nature it cannot be changed by humans. It is embodied in the stories, songs, dances, and paintings about ancestral spirits whose presence in Creation is constant and literal. This mythic view of the world can only adapt at the pace of change in the natural world. The law is therefore immutable. Its application as a literal doctrine by the Ngarinyin has resulted in their inability to resist or successfully adapt to the creativity and intellect, the ability to abstract, analyze, synthesize, and project, and the arts and skills of control and domination that characterize Triangle Thinking. On the other hand, Triangle Thinking, in its current expression, is unsustainable because it fails to reflect, incorporate, or respond to the reality of natural law with its primary doctrine of relationship. Consequently, Triangle Thinking is fundamentally out of balance, limited as it is to a masculine, "right-handed" interpretation of the world. Without a fully recognized and incorporated feminine, Triangle Thinking is inherently nonregenerative and therefore decadent.

Mowaljarlai and I used the symbols of Pattern Thinking and Triangle Thinking to explain to our respective cultures how the relationship between them has been expressed with particular reference to land and land use. Land is fundamental to identity and law in all cultures. Land names people, gives them status and authority, and sustains them in body, mind, and spirit. Coming to terms with the ways in which this most profound of relationships is manifested and expressed in different cultural philosophies is potentially the stuff of conflict or reconciliation and healing. In Australia, this conflict has raged for two decades, and continues to be the most potentially divisive *or* uniting issue of the century.

The pathway of reconciliation and healing is what Mowaljarlai and I named "Two-Way Thinking."

We developed the embryo of this new, Two-Way Thinking model using the dynamics of our own peculiar relationship as a model. We are, after all, man and woman, black and white, Pattern Thinker and Triangle Thinker, and yet we conducted a rich and mutually enhancing friendship for more than two decades without conflict. Adoption of Men's Business, Women's Business principles came first because, in some ways, it was the easiest and most blatantly obvious difference between us. Our color difference was irrelevant except when we were in public together. Through our shared discourse, I contributed the arts of intellect, reading and writing, my skills in logic and reason, analysis, synthesis, and abstraction—in other words, my Triangle Thinking. Mowaljarlai contributed the literal worldview, its language and mythic imagery, his knowledge and practice of the Law of Relationship in its applications within his culture, and countless pieces of evidence from the natural world. There was a humorous irony within this division of thinking skills and styles. His contribution was essentially feminine, and mine was masculine, his from his right-brained, visual dreamworld, and mine from my left-brained, systematic, analytical and classifying world. In these respects, we recognized that Ngarinyin is a right-brain, feminine culture while mine is a left-brain, masculine culture. This convinced us that Two-Way Thinking could, in fact, be a balanced paradigm that could once again reflect the Law of Relationship.

Virtually all productive land in Australia has been taken over for agriculture, mining, or urban uses. This was done quite efficiently and quickly, considering the East Coast was colonized only two hundred years ago. With the exception of pastoral leases, titles that give grazing rights only to the lessees, only the semiarid and arid lands in the center and north of the continent remain undeveloped. Everywhere else in Australia, tribal law and culture have been all but extinguished except for the spiritual attachment to the land which can never be erased. Traditional culture, and the approximately twenty-five thousand tribal Aborigines still remaining in it, all live or maintain Law in these remote, arid, almost pristine traditional homelands. Few Whitefellas occupy or even visit this country. The future of these lands is the subject of current debate in the Australian political arena. The federal government has drafted a legal statute to extinguish completely, or subjugate totally, indigenous Native Title in favor of European land use, whether that use is current, proposed, or even unspecified. If the Australian government is successful, it will effectively disinherit the oldest continuous culture on Earth. The political argument is that there must be clarity in terms of land management, and security for pastoralists and miners to conduct their economic activities for the benefit of the whole nation. The price for this is the destruction of living, tribal Aboriginal Law and culture. The Ngarinyin people, their Law, and their culture are subject to the outcome of whatever the political climate determines.

The paradigm of European Australia is the Triangle Thinking model, so cocultural coexistence is evidently not a politically feasible option because absolute authority over all lands, with power vested in the state, is all that this model can conceive. However, the Ngarinyin and other traditional peoples believe that Two-Way Thinking is not only possible but desirable for the health and well-being of the land and the nation as a whole. They, and a growing number of European Australians, prefer the development of a model that, for the first time in Australia's short history, legally recognizes that Aboriginal Law and culture is a dynamic, living human system that can beneficially coexist with Western Law and culture. Rather than one law being engulfed and consumed by the other, the two can operate together in a synergistic relationship of Pattern Thinking *and* Triangle Thinking.

The principles of this proposed relationship are well established in Ngarinyin and other indigenous Law. The conversion of the literal expression of the Law of Relationship to an abstract paradigm for coexistence would be the task of Two-Way-Thinking westerners in concert with Two-Way-Thinking Aborigines.

The last three chapters of this book expand the Law of Relationship beyond Men's Business, Women's Business to its application in the world at large. Because Ngarinyin and Western cultures have such fundamentally different underlying philosophies, their laws are very different. Each law is rooted in its own mythology. On the one hand, Ngarinyin Law sustained a viable and thriving human social order of hunters and gatherers for tens of thousands of years. On the other, Western law has responded to the increasingly challenging demands of concentrated agglomerates of urban settlement dwellers and the agricultural and industrial development needed to support them. Ngarinyin Law embodies Pattern Thinking exclusively because that is all that has ever been necessary. Western law embodies Triangle Thinking, and because it is a man-made system of management and control, it is able to respond to civilization's rapid changes on demand. The next chapter gives an overview of the application of both systems of law and their philosophical origins, applications, and limitations.

The final chapter is dedicated to sharing two areas where Two-Way Thinking is currently being explored. Seven years ago, when the old Ngarinyin Lawmen and Lawwomen sat down to talk about the plight of their people, they asked themselves, "Which generation do we save?" They decided that they would start with the young ones, those who were as yet undamaged by the ravages of Western culture. The pathway of convergence that is being taken by the Ngarinyin elders, in concert with a group of Whitefellas called Friends of the Ngarinyin, is itself driven by Two-Way Thinking, as are each of the initiatives they are addressing. As we move in this stream of cocultural reconciliation it is becoming increasingly evident that the basic premise was correct. Both cultures and peoples are reaping the rewards of this new, cross-cultural relationship, not only in predicted ways but in ways that were not projected and could not even have been imagined.

Christina Kennedy

Jillian Bangmorra and her mother Susan Collier at Nagomorra, Susan's father's Wunggud place where his spirit derived from a large cloud rock. Bush University.

Chapter Nine

Law in the Mythic

Susan described the land with that kind of thorough detail only found in lifers—people who have wrestled with the moods and vagaries of a land that is constantly trying to reject their efforts in an attempt to restore itself to itself. She told stories of struggle and hardship, of coming to terms with the patterns and shapes of river valleys, swamps, mountains, and gorges, of the limitations of ancient, impoverished soils, and annually renewing floodplains, of plagues and pestilence, of the tyranny of distance, and the ignorance of remote government. Cattle people, irrigation farmers—lifers whose fortunes are made and unmade by nature herself. She revealed a toughness and wisdom that springs from a deep respect born of living with the land.

It is just daylight as we drive our twelve Bush University guests from Kununurra through the great Ord River irrigation area, through vast, million-acre cattle stations, through the history of a century's conquering and conquered pioneers. In the great Australian pioneering tradition this was Susan's country. For years she had been First Lady of the Kimberley until she and her husband were ousted by the acquisitive, ruthless new morality of checkbook power, and remote, disinterested corporate control.

Then I tell my story of the land. Not really my story but the Ngarinyin story which has become part of me, giving me a new sight with which to receive the world. I tell of rounded bodies—breasts, bellies, and thighs—which appear softly in the shadows of new daylight, voluptuous and warm. I relate tales of immense crocodiles and serpents which snake under the skin of the Earth, occasionally rupturing through in vibrant, red-ochre boulders, mesas, and chasms. I point out boab trees, women in all ages and stages of life who cluster together or stand alone, reminders of the full cycle of womanhood. Then there is Daughter Sun who rises above the horizon to reflect her beauty and life in nature's growth.

We turn off the blacktop to travel on a thin ribbon of graded land called the Gibb River Road. We cross riverbeds of rounded stone, sandy creeks, around thighs and shoulders to rest under generous, protective rivergum trees. Daughter Sun is bitten by the snake at midday, and we truck along in quiet awe, vibrating down the corrugated road. As we cross the Drysdale River, a King Brown snake stops our truck in its tracks. We clamber out for a cautious, closer look. "In Ngarinyin belief, this represents a statement by Wunggud, a revelation of the Law," I say. Humbled, everyone returns to the vehicle, and we continue in silence.

We reach our destination at the remote bush camp of Marunbabidi, after Daughter Sun's late afternoon collapse from the tree fork. The old Lawmen greet us with, "Snake has crossed your path. You are welcome here. We must now look after you proper way. That is our Law."

Imagine a world with no written language, and no number system for measurement, no paper or books, and no clocks or rulers. In such a world, how could knowledge be communicated between people? How could law and history be recorded for the benefit of current and future generations? And how could law be understood, and administered? To live in this world, even imaginally, is to experience life as Ngarinyin people have lived it for tens of thousands of years. This is a journey not simply into another culture's material world of being and doing but into a way of thinking and seeing by pathways previously untraveled.

This world, as ancient as the history of the human race and as modern as the contemporary high-tech world of science and the computer chip, has much to teach in the ways of synthesizing the world, and the maintenance and perpetuation of law and order in cultural life. Theirs is a story of belonging in Creation, of living strictly in accordance with natural law. For the Ngarinyin, the world is received and transmitted through direct communication with nature, understood in ritual through performing and visual arts, and consolidated into laws of being and doing through the medium of dream in readily accessible altered states of consciousness. In order to experience the world through these media you must suspend your more familiar intellectual thinking in favor of sensory receptivity, awareness, and responsiveness. Above all, you must observe nature mindfully, listen to the elements carefully, and receive knowledge subjectively.

Ngarinyin Law is not man-made. Rather it is constantly evident in the dual essence of the natural world. Ngarinyin Law is the Law of the sacred revealed in the daily life of ancestral beings who are present in the landscape, in nature, and in art forms. These beings cannot be ignored, their stories cannot be forgotten, and the Law that they generate cannot be changed. To do so would be to profane the sacred. And that, to the Ngarinyin, is tantamount to reducing the true meaning of life to a man-made construct. Law in the mythic realm is therefore absolute and absolutely inviolate.

The basic principle that underlies all Ngarinyin belief is that in all of Creation there are always two energies in relationship with each other. They assert that this is the only way Creation can live. Each of these related energies has a name, and is separate and distinctive, different from the other. Neither exists on its own because both are necessary for the other to live. They give each other life and it is their relationship that matters. The energies are male and female, man and woman, masculine and feminine.

All Law reflects this Law of Relationship.

Ngarinyin Law, which embodies this Law of Relationship, is best revealed through sacred song.

Wunggud

In the beginning all is Wunggud.
All is *of* Wunggud—
its creative power and intent.
Through its own intent
Wunggud reflects itself into form
to continuously form the world.
The world comes into being
as Reflection.
Where the waters above meet the waters below—
at this intersection,
the idea of Creation takes form.
These are the Wunggud Waters,
where the sacred Relationship of
Above and Below
Dance the world into life,
taking the form of Creation—
Reflections.
In the medium of sacred water
idea is reflected into conception.
Through the medium of sacred water
new life is reflected into birth.
By the medium of sacred water
the world is reflected into shape.
All is in Sacred Relationship,
the Pattern of Life,
Wunggud reflected into
the Law of Wurnan.
Each reflection—rock, tree, grass,
animal, and man—
is in Sacred Relationship,
according to the Law—
the pattern, shape, and form of Wunggud.
All is given life,
and powered by Wunggud.
The Pattern itself is
Reflection of Wunggud.

The day is clear and sunny with bright blue skies. Not even the Harvest Spiritmen gather on the horizon as clouds. The families are leaving for a picnic at one of their favorite fishing places, the home of Nagomorra, the freshwater turtle. This was the site of the big meeting of the Wandjina when they came from the north, south, east, and west to discuss the behavior of the two boys who taunted Dumby the Law Owl. It is a good fishing place where black bream abound. As they approach the waterhole, the men stop, call the children over, and point to a hole in the ground on the edge of which are some large, perfectly ovoid, shiny stones. Here the mythic, ancestral freshwater turtle dug into the Earth to lay her eggs. The hole is her burrow, and the stones are the living eggs that she laid. She burrowed through the Earth coming out in the waterhole just below the powerful rock shelter where, with Wandjina, she became a painting.

Most of the group settles down to fish while others swim in the waterhole looking for turtle. The water is smooth and clear. Pandanus palms, rivergums, and spear grass are mirrored in the water, reflections of the world surrounding the Wunggud water that gives them life. So glassy is the surface that, at its edges, they seem joined with each other. Seed pods, spawn, microscopic spores, and organisms skim the water, making slight ripples without bursting its glistening, taut membrane. Beneath the surface is blackness, reaching down into the depths of the unknowable. Here, under the clear blue sky, heaven and Earth unite at the water's surface, joined in reflected acknowledgment of each other. As the hunters and gatherers return to the fire with their catches, an old man lifts his head slightly as if sniffing something in the air. A slight gust of wind chills the sweat on his face and he looks up. Pointing to a shimmering wisp of cloud, the man tells the children to watch. As they look into the sky, the wisp becomes more defined, and then it starts to grow. Elsewhere in the sky, other tiny suggestions of fluff appear and become solid. As the day progresses, more light, puffy clouds appear in the sky. They grow, change shape, and grow some more, all the while moving in and around each other like the gentle dance movements of a ballet—coming together, separating, swirling and twirling in pirouettes, embracing each other in an enfolding harmony. Soon, the cloud ballet becomes a drama. Heavier, loftier movements are danced by stronger, darker clouds which gradually engulf and absorb all the puffy little ones. The man tells the children to be aware, to be mindful of what they observe. Wunggud is showing itself before their very eyes. From nothing visible in the sky, the clouds have appeared to grow and change. Organic and dynamic, the heavens are danced into life and form powered by Wunggud's energies of heat and wind, the agents of heavenly change interacting with each other and the Earth. This is a revelation of Wunggud. And as the sky changes texture, shape, color, temperature, and atmosphere, so its reflection in the Earth changes everything on the Earth. Lively shadows cast their darkness in pockets causing lizards, snakes, and birds to shift in search of warmth. The living wind bristles its shoulders, causing birds to cry out and fly off. The light mood of the families also reflects the change in the atmosphere, becoming more somber, more directed, reflecting the feel of the day. They pack up to leave for their camp.

Reflections

All of Creation is a cycle.
Rocks, trees, plants, animals,
everybody who lives,
has come into being through Wunggud
and returns to Wunggud
in the cycle of
birth, life, death.
In the cycle of life there is growth.
In growth there is change.
In change there is learning.
In learning there is responsibility.
In responsibility there is meaning.
In meaning there is fulfillment.
In fulfillment there is completion.
In completion there is death.
We are Reflections of Nature,
and Nature's cycles.

Like the frog
we change from idea to egg,
from egg to tadpole,
from tadpole to frog,
from frog to mystic,
from mystic, to Nature we return—
this life complete, we return—
to the Earth,
to Wunggud.
We and Nature are Reflections.
Like the tree.
From idea to seed,
from seed to sapling,
from sapling to tree,
in tree to flower,
from flower to death,
to return to the Earth,
to Wunggud.
Our bodies reflect the Earth.
The Earth reflects our bodies.
Our lives reflect the seasons,
the seasons reflect our lives.
The heavens reflect our spirits,
our spirits reflect the heavens.
All live in the spiraling power
of Creation, of Wunggud.

As they leave their picnic place, skirting the waterhole toward the track home, a child lingers at the water's edge, gazing into its shadowy depths. She has seen a movement in the shallows that captivates her. Bounded by lily pads whose flower stalks reach up to the sky, a large tree root stretches down the bank into the water. A frog sits cheekily just above the waterline on the root, its throat gluggily swallowing air and information. Beneath the water's surface, a dozen tadpoles graze hungrily on algae growing on the root. They don't know that they will one day be frogs, and yet that is their destiny. They cannot imagine what the frog's world is like, yet their bodies have all that knowledge. At this stage of their life cycle, they are in full command of their watery environment, and do not see the frog sitting above them, above the water, breathing the air that would kill them. They know only that their entire lives, lived in a continuous present, right where they are at this moment. The child, like the tadpole, knows only her world as a child. When her aunt comes to see what has caught her attention, the young girl points to the tadpoles. Her aunt points to the frog and explains that one day all of those little swimming babies will grow legs, their tails will be absorbed into their bodies, and they will climb out of the security of the water into the new world of air. When they do this, they become Banman, or mediums, able to live in both air and water, able to receive and send messages between the worlds. But they will never forget who they are, and how they came to be frogs. For now, this frog keeps watch over the tadpoles even though they are apparently unaware of his presence or his duty to them. The woman takes the child by the hand and leads her off in the direction of the group.

The breeze stretches its muscles and strengthens to wind. Far away in the distance, just above the horizon, a spear of lightning zaps the ground. Its faint, rumbling growl is heard some time later. Everybody notices the message, and waits for the next strike. They see a single thunderhead appearing like a giant gray blue funnel, frayed at its edges, connecting heaven and Earth. The jagged, streaking spear appears again, and the women gather the children closer. It is far away still and may not travel in their path, but they still heed its passage. This is Wandjina issuing forth in fiery power to meet the filament spat up by the Banman frog from its Wunggud waterhole. Spurting rain from his cloud into the indentations in the Earth made by the Wunggud Snake in Creation time, Wandjina renews and replenishes the seminal waters of life with his issue. Another thunderhead becomes visible and it seems to be on a path that converges with the first. This time, the rumble is felt as a deep vibration in the sandy ground, a warning to the travelers to be alert. Squawking black cockatoos fly overhead as sinking Daughter Sun is blotted out temporarily, sucking the color out of the land. The old man points out to the children the huge bowl-like haloes that radiate from the thunderheads, concentric circles that reach out over the sky to be reflected in the shadows of the Earth and the ripples in the waterhole. Wandjina visits all his seminal seed places as he has done since Creation time when he first walked the Earth to leave imprints of himself in rock shelters and remind the tribes of his presence and their responsibilities. Wandjina lies down in Creation to make sure everybody keeps the Law.

Wandjina

Creation time,
Lai Lai it is called,
when Wandjina came with the light,
daylight, to form the land.
As Wandjina brought life into being,
when the land was soft like a jelly,
he rested.
In those resting places,
near the Wunggud waters
he became a painting.
Wandjina imprinted himself in the caves
to mark the places
where he brought life into being—
all of Creation,
one by one,
each place being the story
in the land form.
Wandjina spirit is in the land
wherever Wandjina roamed.
His journey is marked by his imprints
where he left himself.
Within the inside of the boundary
of all his living memorials,
he lies down in the land—
Wandjina himself is lying down
within the arc of himself in the land.
Each Wandjina revelation sings its own song,
its own story,

and is known by the evidence where the created
became a painting,
a sculpture in the land,
a continuously visited increase site.

The families decide to stop in a shelter until the storms pass. As they
sit around the rocks and in the sand, the old man tells a story. In early
times, a Banman called Wibalma made sacred objects. This was before
the Law. He kept these objects in his workplace, and didn't let anyone
else have them. He didn't want to share his power with anybody, he
just wanted to keep it all for himself. One day while he was out
hunting, two heroes, Wodoi and Djingun, came to his camp to see him.
"Where is Wibalma?" they asked his wife. She told them that he was
out hunting. Wibalma's wife was blind so she did not recognize them.
And she did not see what they did next. Wodoi and Djingun went
quietly to Wibalma's workplace, stole a sacred object, and fled. Wibalma,
who was a really powerful Banman, suspected something bad was
happening with a sacred object so he hurried back to his camp. When
he discovered what had been stolen he was very angry. So angry that
he picked up his boomerang and hurled it at an ironwood tree,
splitting it right down the middle. This made all the sacred objects
stand up.

Wibalma took off after the thieves, following their tracks. When he
came to the sand plains, he could no longer find their tracks. He
looked and looked but he could see nothing. So he went up higher to
the rocky ground, the stone lines where he found some telltale marks
which told him he was back on their trail. He couldn't find their tracks
in the open, sandy ground. He could only see their tracks when they
were in the rock. He could follow the power of that sacred object only
one way, in rock.

Wodoi and Djingun did not want it that way. They wanted a
sharing of power, a sharing Law of sand and rock—the power in
stone lines and the power of the sandy space in between. They
wanted to put this shared power in the Wurnan, the Law of Relationship. So Wodoi, that spotted nightjar bird, and Djingun, the owlet
nightjar, decided to make a new Law, the Law of Wurnan. They made

an agreement to prepare a sacrifice for initiating their new Law. Wodoi went out and got emu for his sacrifice. Djingun, who arrived back first, brought sugarbag or wild bush honey. When Wodoi arrived at their camp he found Djingun cooking the sugarbag. It was dripping all over the coals. "You can't cook honey!" exclaimed Wodoi. "You should have brought back raw flesh for a blood sacrifice!" Wodoi hit Djingun hard on the head, knocking him down. Frightened, Wodoi ran away. Djingun soon recovered and followed Wodoi, tracking him down. When he found Wodoi, he hit him so hard on the head that his blood poured into the ground. Wodoi's sacrificial blood is the red ochre. After that, they decided to make peace with each other. That white pipe clay of Djingun, with no blood, that's the peace clay. That's why we always have red and white paint for dancing.

Wodoi and Djingun arrived in their community with this new Law. Wibalma, who caught up with them there, accepted this new idea of sharing power. A council meeting was held and everybody agreed that from now on marriage would be based on this new Law, so Wodoi daughters can only marry Djingun sons, and Djingun daughters can only marry Wodoi sons. That way, everything is shared, right down the middle, two ways. That's why everybody and everything is either Wodoi or Djingun. All the land follows these lines. All of nature follows those lines in a big relationship map of Creation with everything in its place. And that is how Wurnan started, and lives today. Those sacrificial stones mark the spot where Wodoi and Djingun made their covenant. And the Law table, where the council of all the clans from the north, south, east, and west meet, is where the kinship lines still go out today.

Wurnan

In all of Creation there are always two.
In Wurnan there are always two.
In Wunggud there are always two.
Wodoi and Djingun are the two laws
that, together, are the Law.

143

Wodoi—bones	Djingun—dust
Wodoi—hunters	Djingun—gatherers
Wodoi—hunted	Djingun—gathered
Wodoi—men	Djingun—women
Wodoi—women	Djingun—men
Wodoi—father	Djingun—mother
Wodoi—children	
Wodoi—mother	Djingun—father
	Djingun—children
Wodoi—Executioner	Djingun—Life-giver
Wodoi—brolga	Djingun—turtle
Wodoi—land	Djingun—land
Wodoi—rock	Djingun—sand
Wodoi—red ochre	Djingun—white clay pipe
Wodoi—animal blood	Djingun—vegetable
Wodoi—spotted nightjar	Djingun—owlet nightjar

Everything in Creation is named
Wodoi and Djingun.
Always two—
that is the Law.
Like the reeds
woven into a basket.
Masculine uprights, the warp:
Feminine weave, the weft.
Not one without the other.
The basket, a tapestry of Wurnan.
The idea of the form,
and the energy that holds the form,
that infuses the reeds,
that gives the shape,
the weaving and the woven—
that is Wunggud
in Wurnan.

Satisfied that the storms will present no danger to the group, that Wandjina is not punishing them, the men decide to leave the shelter, and lead the way out across the sand plain followed by the women. The men always lead while traveling and women always follow, tending the children as they go. The men carry spears, and the woomera slinging tool which is named after its prototype, the fork of a young tree. The women carry their digging sticks named after the kingfisher bird who burrows into the riverbank to lay her eggs. Everything is named from its mythic source, the stories of which are regularly told as the older people introduce the world to the young. Men tell men's stories, women tell women's stories. The Law governing Men's Business and Women's Business is found in nature, the biological reality of life. What constitutes a man is reflected in his function. What constitutes a woman is reflected in her function. Strict delineation of function flows naturally from the mindful observation and awareness of the natural order. The stories that are told associate all aspects of Creation, seen and unseen, with their ancestral past, giving meaning to a continuing present.

Awareness of the Law is not the result of an intellectual understanding. It does not come from books, the written word, or from measuring and proving the world. It is the product of living mindfully in the continuing presence of the sacred in which the ancestral past constantly presents itself as reality. Nature itself is the teacher, reflected in the spirits, minds, and bodies of men and women who learn to recognize the sacred images, functions, and meanings. From the tiniest protozoan to the eternal landscape and the great cosmic dome, the reflected images of male and female are recognized through stories of mythic heroes and heroines, of great adventures, and in acts of Creation. These are recalled, renewed, and celebrated in daily rituals, actions based on beliefs, divinations, foretellings, song, and dance. The images are present as living entities in the natural sculptures of the land. They have painted themselves on stone. One learns about the world through dynamic experiences in which all of Creation are players. All authority begins and ends here, in the living Mythic of the ancestral past simultaneously alive in Creation's present.

Creation

The Earth is the Body—
our bodies are reflections
of the Earth.
In the Earth are all body parts
which give our body parts their power.
All body parts are Relationship,
connected by energy meridians
through which flows the life force,
the weave of Creation,
of which we are reflections.
The Earth's body gives our bodies
their substance,
their form,
their functions,
their meaning.
The Earth is Mother,
gestating, birthing, renewing life.
The Pattern of the Earth is Father,
giving Law and structure to life.
The Earth is Husband
who inseminates life.
The Earth is Wife who carries our children.
The Earth is all our kinship
in the Pattern of Life.
We and the Earth are woven together,
Belonging in each other,
Reflections, energetically connected.
Like the image in the waters
one cannot be without the other;
there are always two.
Male body reflects male power
while holding sacred, She.
Female body reflects female power
while holding sacred, He.
Woman reflects She to Man.

Man reflects He to Woman.
This way they are bonded together
in sacred, reflective Relationship,
within and without,
in Wurnan.
Women are the Womb of Creation.
Men are the Activators of Life.
Women do "inside" business,
a reflection of their bodies.
Men do "outside" business,
a reflection of their outside bodies.
Together in sacred Relationship
they are the warp and weft,
the weavers and the woven
of life, of kinship, of replenishment.
Wodoi and Djingun,
there are always Two.

Imagine a world in which all Law and knowledge is encoded in written and spoken languages, and is stored on paper or in digital books. In this world, there are two primary language systems—word and number. These are intellectual constructs that, in accordance with strict rules governing their interpretation and use, determine, define, describe, and, where possible, measure everything that is known to exist. To access, reproduce, or communicate this knowledge and law, people must first learn how to use these two systems in both spoken and written forms, and adhere strictly to their rules. It is exclusively through competent use of these systems that the people of this world are able to share knowledge and Law. But it is only through the achievement of highly developed intellectual and written skills that academic qualifications and authority can be achieved.

This is the world of logos, the intellectual, reasoned world of human consciousness and its contemporary products—scientific materialism, economic rationalism, and political idealism. In this world, the literate and numerate view themselves as superior to the rest of

Creation. The small percentage of those who are bestowed with man-made academic qualifications assume an additional godlike right to manage and modify any part or all of the natural order to serve their own, and what they believe to be others' human interests. It is a worldview based on the assumptions that, according to scientism: the primary unit of existence is the single unit, separate and distinct from all other single units; there is a hierarchy of value within the natural order of which literate and numerate human beings are at the top; among human beings, the male gender is superior to the female; the highest form of knowledge is scientific, objective, measurable, and therefore provable; and the highest human potential is found in the academically developed intellect. All Law, knowledge, and authority hang on these man-made constructs.

Creation

God said, "Let us make man in our own image,
in the likeness of ourselves,
and let them be masters of the fish of the sea,
the birds of heaven, the cattle,
all the wild beasts
and all the reptiles that crawl upon the earth."
God created man in the image of himself,
in the image of God he created him,
male and female he created them.
God blessed them, saying to them,
"Be fruitful, multiply, fill the earth and conquer it.
Be masters of the fish of the sea,
the birds of heaven
and all living animals on the earth."

Gen. 1:26–28

However, what I want you to understand
is that Christ is the head of every man,
man is the head of woman,
and God is the head of Christ. . . .
A man should certainly not cover his head,

since he is the image of God
and reflects God's glory;
but woman
is the reflection of man's glory.
For man did not come from woman;
no, woman came from man;
and man was not created for the sake of woman,
but woman was created for the sake of man.

1 Cor. 11:3, 7–10

In the second millennium, Western culture's creed has all but completed the act of separation from the sacred. When applied in the sciences of the intellect, the logical, the objective, and the rational have made the previously sacred become profane. The divine authority of God is dead, seemingly replaced by the secular authority of the laws of logos. Or is it?

Humanity once received its knowledge and Law from direct communications with nature. This was followed historically by the foretellings of prophets. The next stage in man's development of consciousness was text-based teachings mediated by a priesthood which claimed divine authority and demanded obedience to themselves and the Word. With the decline of the authority of the priesthood, those very teachings have been relegated to the status of an optional personal creed. Religious teachings are banned from the secular classrooms of education, are considered redundant as a basis for law, have no role or status whatever in the affairs of state, and are considered completely irrelevant to science.

The campfire casts images of the gods onto the faces of the young boys who poke at its vitality with sticks. They are telling each other stories in the last hour of a birthday party which celebrates the eleventh year of one of the boys. One boy pulls his lighted stick from the fire and starts to wave it around, releasing its fire-fairies to the cold night air. Another warns, "Eeh! You shouldn't do that! We're not allowed to do that. You might attract the spirits of dead people. You might call them into here." This child is Aboriginal. A twelve-year-old

Thai lad sitting next to the fire thrower agrees, saying that they are not allowed to do that either. The firestick-wielding lad says dismissively, "*Pffst . . .* what rubbish. It's only fire! Spirits aren't true anyway!"

Silenced, the Aboriginal boy hangs his head. At that instant, the smoldering, red end of the stick flies off, landing on the leg of its wielder. Startled, he looks at the Aboriginal boy as if suspecting an act of sorcery or magic.

Their stories turn to real and imagined brushes with the spirit world. As if validated by this new, energetic interest, the Aboriginal lad tells of many experiences, characteristics, behaviors, and evidence of an ever-present mythic reality. The boys listen, entranced. By now he is standing, his whole body immersed in the action and energy of his story subjects, his voice modulating with the expressions and tones of the living drama he is sharing. As his storytelling comes to a close, he looks at his guardian, seeking affirmation that what he told is the truth. His guardian relates an experience she and a group of Whitefellas shared while in the boy's country on a camping trip. She tells of a dingo howl that woke everyone from the heaviness of deep slumber in the middle of the night. As the visitors emerged from their tents, they were startled at the sight of thousands of the tiniest lights floating in the air about head height from the ground, each of them leaving a gossamer vapor trail, weaving and ducking in and around each other. The visitors were told that the lights were the Dancing Ri, the spirits of the primordial swamp on which they were camping. The dingo was howling up the spirit people, heralding that a spirit baby had been dreamed into one of the visitors.

Immediately the firestick boy scoffs. "That 's stupid!" he exclaims. He adds vehemently that babies don't come from any dancing spirits. Everybody knows that babies come from the man and woman having sex, when he puts his seed inside her to fertilize an egg. He knows this because his dad told him. And his dad tells him only the truth, never make-believe stories or other lies. And his dad knows all of these things because he is a lawyer *and* a mathematician so he's a pretty smart man. After a pause in conversation, the same boy asks the guardian, "Is it really true? Did you really see those spirit things?" She replies that she has really seen them, and yes, they are true because a lady who had been trying to have a baby for ten years became pregnant soon after returning to her home. Shattered, the boy takes his experience home to his father who carefully explains to his son that, while we don't believe those stories because we know from medical science how babies are really made, we listen courteously and respectfully to those who do. The boy will learn the details of the chemistry, biology, and physiology of making babies in school because schools are allowed to teach about the world only with real, provable knowledge, not through myth, superstition, or fantasy.

The emergence of intellectual consciousness in Western and, to a lesser extent, other cultures has carried with it the demise of the authority of the Divine, and the feminine. As the great patriarchal religions, their deities, priesthoods, and teachings are marginalized, man-made secular systems of authority struggle to bind the hearts and minds of the populace in a quasi-religious sense of nationhood. The Ten Commandments of the Judeo-Christian tradition have been replaced by the state's one thousand and one legislative commandments as governments made out of men attempt to emulate the now discredited powers and laws of the Earth, the Goddess, and God. By the exclusive application of rational consciousness, and the ideological principles of the logos's new mythologies, prayer has been supplanted by education, sacramental holy communion with food and nutrition, ecclesiastical preaching with political ideology, compassion with invasive modern medicine, and the laws of nature with the laws of reason. The Word is now millions of books of words.

The highest court in the nation meets to consider whether Aboriginal people have any legal entitlement to land that was colonized by the British two hundred years ago. At stake is a vast area of the continent whose primary cultural occupation and use is, in the present time, indigenous—people whose living Law and heritage date back to time immemorial. The court's deliberations are thorough as they consider all relevant national and international legal statutes and principles of law. Their conclusion is that the indigenous people of Australia do have prior claim to lands and waters where they can demonstrate continuous culture.

The federal government then set about creating a legal statute to define and regulate what they now call Native Title.

Many months, then years, pass without any Native Title being legally validated by the courts despite the best efforts of many groups of indigenous people. One group of old tribal Lawmen, denied access to money to support their legal case for Native Title, decided to be their own lawyers. After all, they are fully qualified and acknowledged Lawmen in their own culture, and know the meaning of Native Title better than any academically qualified Lawmen in the national legal system. This decision causes a flurry of concern in the institutional ranks of lawyers. How will they present their evidence? Can they speak English? How can they possibly understand the complexities of the legal system and points of law?

The tribal Lawmen have no alternative but to present their knowledge and Law in the only way they know—through storytelling, dance, song, ritual, and ceremony, by showing their Law written in the land, and scarred into their bodies.

Commissioners and judges confer. Politicians confer. The media are baffled, confronted by their own ignorance and difficulty in understanding the Lawmen's spoken English. The old men are illiterate and innumerate in English, and have no written language of their own. It is decided by the authorities that evidence must be written in words; anthropological reports must be submitted; only material evidence will be allowed; and no spiritual evidence can be allowed because it cannot be subjected to the rigors of objective scrutiny. The politicians review the Native Title Act, making sure that no possible interpretation would liberate indigenous people from the constraints of the one true law of the land, the only law that can endow exclusive land title.

Another year passes, and still no Native Title is formally granted. The vested political and economic interests of the land unite as one front, seeking to extinguish Native Title where there might be grasses for cattle to graze, minerals to explore and exploit, scenery to attract tourists, fish to catch, and waters to dam before a single significant case appears in court. A ten-point plan is created by the political ideologues and the economic rationalists, a plan that effectively diminishes Native Title, like divine authority, to a memory, a remnant of its original intent. This is done in favor of nonindigenous economic development, and the perpetuation of ownership and control in the hands of the vested financial and political institutions. The old tribal Lawmen shake their heads, saying, "Our Law is written in the land. We can't change that Law. It lasts for as long as the land lasts. Your law is written on paper. You mob change your law all the time. You can just crush it up and chuck it out anytime. How can you ever know who you really are?"

The laws of man have extinguished subtlety, imagery, parable, and mythic events until we are left with only text-based academic constructs that are accessible only to those with special training in their unique and particular languages. The languages and laws of the mythic, whose words and authorities nourish, inspire, motivate, and sustain the individual and collective human spirit, are now relegated to the margins of social life and community consciousness. A student of dance may not dance her thesis into life, an artist may not paint or sculpt his beliefs into a formal acknowledgment, a musician may not be recognized as a master without the stamp of approval from an academic institution. A storyteller may not become a master at all. The world is now formally presented in theoretical frameworks whose parameters are defined by their capacity to be objectified, reasoned, and measured. Poetry, music, dance, literary narrative, ritual, and ceremony have been molded into disciplines that can be studied and assessed by standardized methodologies in accordance with the laws of logos. Human passions, yearnings, biological functions, kinship rights and responsibilities, public and private behaviors, thoughts, words, and deeds are now all governed by statute law, violations of which bring punishments of incarceration or other privation. The laws of the state penetrate deeply into everyone's awareness and consciousness. Legislatures around the Western world add hundreds of new laws to their statutes every year in an effort to regulate and control an extraordinary and diverse range of human behaviors previously governed by shared religious values and codes of conduct. The human spirit is not, however, easily or readily contained within rules not rooted in the numinous.

It is getting late on this beautiful summer night, the day's crackling heat now subdued to warm earth and wind. Young people have been gathering at the beach since sunset for swimming, chatting in groups, wandering across the road through the car park to the pub for a drink, then back to the beach. These days are always lazy, just made for fun and laughter. As night draws on, many reluctantly leave for homes that they know will have trapped the day's hot air to spend a stifling, probably sleepless night. Others stay at the beach, having decided to sleep in the sand dunes.

In the pub, a group of girls laugh at the fact that they have not been picked up for underage drinking. One of the girls starts to feel a bit seedy so she decides to go outside into the fresh air. She starts to walk across the road toward the sand dunes. She realizes that she is quite unsteady on her feet just as a wave of nausea sweeps over her. Four bikers lean on their machines as they share a carton of beer, bawdy jokes, and commentaries on the people coming and going from the bar. They see the girl teeter as she crosses the road, see her lean over ready to be sick. One saunters over to her and asks if she is all right. She tells him that she hadn't realized how much she had to drink, laughing, a little embarrassed. Then she vomits.

The other young men come over to see what is going on. The girl tells them she feels really dizzy, and starts to shake. She thinks she should sit down. But before she can get to a seat, she passes out.

Sometime in the small hours of the morning a youth, unable to sleep in his hot bedroom, goes for a walk along the beach. As he approaches the shore in front of the hotel, he decides to cut across the sand dunes to the car park. A light, muffled whimper startles him and he stops. He does not want to interrupt any couples who are sleeping out this night so he cautiously follows the sound. In the soft moonlight, he finds the girl, bleeding, unable to get up, her clothing scattered around her.

Three months later, the daily newspapers shout their headlines— "PACK RAPE TRIAL: Youths Plead Not Guilty." Over the ensuing days, the full, horrible story unfolds. The young men, their judgment affected by alcohol, had carried the girl into the sand dunes. There, for the next two hours, they masturbated into her limp, lifeless body, several times each. They had engaged in a competition over how long it would take to ejaculate, given that they had been drinking. At the time they thought it was pretty funny because one of them could not, at first, sustain an erection to even enter her. All the while, the girl, still unconscious, had not protested.

She is asthmatic. According to expert medical evidence, it was the combination of her regular medication with the moderate amount of alcohol she had consumed that had caused her to pass out.

Legal argument turns to the question of "consent." The youths pleaded innocence on the grounds that, because she did not object, they believed that her silence constituted assent. The girl's counsel tells of the physical and psychological trauma and suffering that she continues to experience—the unrelenting shame, her sense of culpability, the feeling of "dirtiness" that continues to drive her to wash her body until her flesh bleeds, her inability to make eye contact with males, her withdrawal—not just from her first-year university course, but from society altogether. The judge returns to points of law. As devastating as this experience had undoubtedly been for her, the fact remains that, in law, her suffering can be considered in the deliberation about a sentence only if the court finds the young men guilty. There remained legal argument as to whether or not the men, given their alcohol-induced state of "diminished responsibility," were capable of objective judgment about the girl's condition, and what they understood to be her "assent by silence."

Two weeks of technical legal arguments later, daily newspaper headlines shout "NOT GUILTY" around the nation. A day later, the girl commits suicide.

In Western culture, the human spirit is clearly not satisfied with such man-made authorizations, so much so that the oft-quoted British truism, "The law is an ass," is a regular topic for debate in schools, colleges, and the media. The courtroom has become the "live theater" of high drama with its players achieving both the fame and pay scales of Hollywood stars. Western law now appears to be less the delivery of justice than a public forum in which star professionals compete across a courtroom, pitting their creative application of intellect against each other by manipulating highly technical statutes to achieve a victory. Within this scenario lie the seeds of evidence that human consciousness needs the Mythic.

There is a hunger in humans that drives them to seek authorities beyond the reach of logos. The world of film now inspires humanity to extend itself to its full psychological and spiritual potential. In thousands of magazines around the world, there is a ready bank of mythic heroes and heroines whose characters, life stories, adventures, fortunes, and misfortunes are devoured daily. Artists, dancers, poets, writers, and musicians of all genres provide the contemporary stuff of the creative and Mythic as they offer to nourish, inspire, and inform the public about cultural truths and society's condition. These visual, literary, and performing artists live outside the formal institutions of Western culture. Their only qualification is their popularity among the people themselves. Meanwhile, in the private world of the collective psyche, the human spirit engages in divination with otherworld authorities. Tarot, runes, crystals, channelings, spirit guides, angels, and even modern psychotherapy are all attempts by Western civilization to return to what is no longer there in the world of logos. Through these mediums, adherents find a worldview beyond that offered by man-made authorities. They are given a hierarchy of importance that more closely reflects their inner life. They find definition and guidance about what to do or think. In each instance, adherents receive what religion provided more universally in times past—a comprehensive explanation of what it is to be fully human. The evidence does not end there. Video game parlors provide youth with their own brand of mythic heroes in full action. Fantasy games such as Dungeons and Dragons engage and entrance the young in a mythic reality that they take into their ordinary lives. Reconstructed historical fantasies such as the Arthurian legend have become metaphors for contemporary ceremony and ritual where the magical, mythic authorities of the Merlins and Muses hold the powers that mortals seek to access and politicians attempt to emulate. Even in the field of scientific materialism, the search for the "ultimate formula" for everything has brought seekers full circle back to the fundamentals of nature, and to a realization of just how wrong the pursuit has been.

Jutta Malnic

Mowaljarlai teaching Archbishop Peter Carnley and friends under the images of Wandjina at Nagomorra during Bush University.

Chapter Ten

Converging Paradigms

It was the first time that the boys had traveled out of the Kimberley, and the first time they had flown on a jet aircraft. They arrived in the metropolis of Perth, Western Australia, to be confronted by elevators, moving walkways, and stairs, a bitumen-covered landscape, freeways, traffic lights, noise, smells, bright lights, and the promises of the city. They wore their entire wardrobe of clothes— jeans, T-shirts, and joggers. The two Ngarinyin boys, aged nine and twelve, had come to "the Cities," a dreamworld seen only on television, to fulfill a dream.

I had already bought all the material requirements they needed to start their new life as boarders in a prestigious boys college. Only their school uniforms remained to be fitted. As it was Men's Business to attire the boys, my son supervised them trying on formal uniforms, everyday uniforms, athletic, football, and soccer uniforms, ties, socks, school shoes, various sports shoes, and casual shoes. The previous evening, he had demonstrated the "Gardia" or Whitefella protocols of shaking hands, making eye contact when greeting, the verbal responses to use when communicating with somebody in authority, the art of tying shoelaces and neck ties, and the skill of folding clothes.

Dressed in their everyday uniforms, the boys were conducted to the preparatory school to meet the headmaster with whom we shared a sit-down lunch in the dining room. The headmaster and I realized the Gardia dining protocols had been overlooked, and we noted that fact. After lunch the boys were instructed to go to the boarding house and change out of their uniforms and into their athletic gear. Later they were to change back into their uniforms for the evening meal taken in the main dining room, then into their pajamas and dressing gowns to be ready for sleeping. The boys took in all of these clothes-changing instructions and protocols with bemused bewilderment.

The headmaster arrived to inspect them in their sports attire, and, while congratulating them on their appearance, he told the older boy that he still had on his gray school socks. He must wear white socks for athletics. The boy looked at his feet, looked at the headmaster, removed his joggers and socks, pulled out a pair of white socks from his cupboard, and put them on. As he was retying his laces, he looked up quizzically and asked, "Do white socks run faster?"

It seems incredible that a human culture that has the intelligence and skills to produce the computer chip, conduct molecular surgery, design and service a metropolis of millions of people, and communicate with the stars could also destroy its own ability to survive and thrive as a culture and a society. This paradoxical scenario may seem too fantastic to believe, yet some would claim that the seeds of the destruction of Western culture have not only been planted but are growing vigorously. It is a truism in nature that any species, colony, or ecology in which the female is destroyed, or within which the delicate balance between male and female function is seriously disrupted, cannot thrive. There is ample evidence to support this in human populations and former civilizations whose rises and falls can be plotted using the indicators of relationship balance.

Modern world history amply demonstrates that where male domination and subjugation of culture and nation reign untempered by the influence of the feminine, fatherlands are born while the heart and soul of culture withers. It is perhaps poignant that irrefutable evidence for this view comes from a culture that has experienced this process in just the last ninety years.

In its primary form, Ngarinyin culture has been ravaged and mutilated by Western culture. What the visionary Ngarinyin Lawpeople are bringing to the West's attention is that every step and stage of decline, every single cultural and social issue that has confronted Ngarinyin people in the last sixty or so years, now confronts the peoples of Western society on a global scale. What can be seen and recorded in the decline of indigenous cultures worldwide can now be seen, as if in reflected imagery and process, within the societies of the Western world.

Social breakdown is the end product of dramatic and traumatic changes in the fundamental structures of society and culture that people believed to be sacrosanct. At the turn of the twentieth century, Ngarinyin culture was overtaken by early British colonial culture which assumed the authority to "civilize and Christianize the natives." Inherent in this little phrase were the weapons of absolute destruction of a living social and spiritual order whose grounding lay in the drive and belief that human beings belong within an organic, natural order. They were unable to resist the process of colonization because the invaders rode horses, wielded firepower, and were highly experienced, institutionalized servants of a sovereign rulership made of men.

That same authority has been applied against its own people within Western culture. Even as recently as the turn of the nineteenth century there were organic societies comprised of families, neighborhoods, and communities regulated by a dynamic social and spiritual order and sustained by a living myth. Now there are institutionally regulated and digitally managed networks of amorphous social agglomerates, within which are all the same symptoms of dysfunction and destruction evident within indigenous cultures and societies. That may seem a harsh judgment but the evidence is all there. In every postmodern society, authorities are grappling with epidemic violence against individuals and property, rape and abuse of women, juvenile anarchy, family breakdown, drug abuse, and rising public apathy and cynicism, all of which reflect the dysfunction and agony of humanity's heart and spirit. The Ngarinyin Lawmen recognize the trend because they have seen all of these debilitating social diseases afflict their own people since they came under the power and might of logos in postmodern civilization.

Commentators and visionaries of both cultures issue a grave warning, and offer a brave gift. Humanity in all societies must acknowledge and give life to a fundamental, universal philosophy and to governing principles of relationship, and it must *re*member a profound respect for the sacred.

To achieve this perhaps idealistic commitment is to acknowledge the universal patterns, trends, and details that characterize the human condition in all societies. Then these must be consciously and mindfully reframed, both personally and collectively, to reflect an organic, sustainable paradigm of survival and meaning. As their tens-of-thousands-of-years-old society breaks down, and the old Law disappears with the deaths of its primary custodians, a small group of senior Ngarinyin Lawmen have banded together with a growing international group of Whitefellas to explore the pathway of convergence called Two-Way Thinking.

Bush University

We have a gift we been trying to give you.

We old people in the Law, there's not many of us left now. We're all dying off, or been killed off by alcohol and disease and heartbreak because we're still not in our country, our proper place.

Our gift will give you your meaning, your belonging. We have to give it to you now before our time runs out.

For a long, long time we have been trying to give our gift to you but we are always blocked.

We're blocked by media because they don't know how to talk to us.

We're blocked by university people because they lock up our knowledge. All our evidence has been locked up in universities and museums. Doctoral people write down our evidence in languages that are too hard for anybody to understand. They've written it up so that the meaning is lost. Our gift is not just systems on paper. It is the experience of life.

We're blocked by politicians who are frightened we might lock them out of their power over us. Their fear stops them from listening to us properly, Lawmen to Lawmen.

We're blocked by Gardia law because the rules of law shut up our mouths and only let us speak through Gardia lawyers in courtrooms in cities. Our gift is lost this way because lawyers have to obey Gardia thinking.

We're blocked by Gardia economic development because their mineral wealth is in our country and they don't want to be stopped from getting it out. And pastoralists who let their cattle run all over our sacred space, cutting up the country with their hooves, spoiling our sacred waters, killing off our animals, our totems, our identity. This cattle mob block us from our Law sites, our paintings, where we camp and do our ceremony. They take Gardia tourists to our sites without our permission—without knowing the sacred meaning.

We old people want to tell you this. We want to give you our gift so you can belong properly in this country and not be afraid. We want to fill up your emptiness with meaning so you can respect us and our country. We've been trying for a long time.

This is what we want to do before our time is up.

We want to teach our young people their meaning, their belonging, so they stop getting lost to emptiness and alcohol. We want to teach Gardia young people so they stop killing themselves and getting lost too.

We want to teach all Australians about their belonging in this country so they stop destroying their meaning before it's too late. They're ignorant of what they're doing because they don't know. They can't understand how to relate to land, and how land looks after them if they don't learn these things. We want to teach them that respect.

We want to leave you our heritage. Not in university papers that nobody reads or understands. We want to teach you in our country so you experience what we know.

We can't do any of this while Gardia keep making laws and protests and arguments to keep us out of our proper place. They just run us out of time doing this. We know what we want to do, and we know we have to start our important work now before it's too late and we're dead gone. Everybody will suffer, really suffer if we die before we can give you our gift.

We Ngarinyin have a vision for our country and it is our gift. Bush University is one of the big ideas we want to start.

Already we have filmed a lot of our sacred places and our ceremony, so after we're gone, our children and you have that evidence.

We have already started taking people from the cities and overseas into our country for them to get their meaning.

We want to develop our own communications station in our country, so everybody can talk to us directly, not through somebody else. There are people in America and Germany and Canada trying to contact us to learn from us. We want to teach them.

Our story is being written up in art. This is starting to go out to all the world.

We've been broadcasting on radio for everyone to hear. We're speaking at places where Gardia come to listen, at seminars and conferences. We're talking everywhere to tell people about Ngarinyin culture, Ngarinyin stories, Ngarinyin meaning. Gardia are really enjoying filling up with these stories.

We're doing all this so we can start up our Bush University. White people are crying out to learn about our culture, and we cry because we're blocked from teaching.

The country is not going anywhere. The minerals are not going anywhere. The paintings are not going anywhere. There is plenty of time left for them. Only we are going somewhere. Our time is running out.

DAVID MOWALJARLAI, OAM
speaker, Australian National Native Tribunal Objections Hearing
Marunbabidi Camp, Western Australia, November 1995

They had come from every corner of Australia, and from overseas. An internationally renowned artist, a popular fiction writer, three lawyers, a broadcaster, a Queen's Counsel, and a retired judge, people of old and new wealth. This was an invited group of middle-aged privileged people who could afford to go anywhere in the world for their annual holidays and they chose to accept the invitation to attend the inaugural Bush University at Marunbabidi Camp, home to a group of Ngarinyin people in the Law.

It was the third day—time to prepare lunch and put the corned beef into camp ovens, then onto coals for the evening meal. The visiting women laughed lightly and spoke freely, having returned from the Wunggud waterhole where almost all had touched the sacred, some for the first time. An awakening experience. They shared few words, overpowered by the subtle energies in which they danced. This was no time for intellectual understanding, psychoanalysis, or verbiage. This was the Mythic. They had crossed over into the dreaming, and all were aware of the sweet smell of the seemingly thick air in the golden part of the Wunggud's banks where they shared private Women's Business.

Then they heard the whooping of the returning hunters, the males on the tour who had been out doing Men's Business with the Ngarinyin Lawmen. They had brought down a bush turkey and were ecstatic. The men told of the sighting, the chase, the shot, the second chase, the second shot, and the return to the truck with the handsome, tall bird who had surrendered its life to nourish the visitors. The senior Lawman Neowarra carried it off by the neck, back to the Ngarinyin camp, and put it on a tarp for everyone's inspection. What to do now? "Pluck it," he said to no one in particular. Di the writer and Suzanna the barrister-broadcaster knelt to the task.

Neowarra told them to take off all the feathers so the bird was really clean. The wind would take them away. But the women bagged them for they knew not what purpose. Observers came and went as the plucking continued. Di sat back, ready for someone else to have a turn at plucking and, looking around for the next plucker, realized they had all vanished and that she and Suzanna would complete the task, if a little reluctantly. Neowarra sat, arms folded, smiling face under a Chicago Bulls hat, singing the turkey song. Di and Suzanna turned the bird over, and became silent, totally absorbed in the feathers' styles, shapes, textures, and colors. As Neowarra sang his haunting song, Di changed her relationship with her task and the big bird. She and the bird melded in a relationship of sacrifice and appreciation. Her pluck-ing became a ritual, a sacred experience, and her face transformed. At that moment, she ceased to be a visitor trying out indigenous experi-ences. She became the experience directly, as it had been for thousands of years in that place. She was no different from the women before her who, for millennia, had plucked the bird in grateful reverence. She became one with indigenous women doing Women's Business.

She and Suzanna continued in the process of preparing the bird for cooking. Next they cut its throat, removed its legs, slit its guts to remove the bowel, stomach, liver, heart, and intestines, washed all the parts, and cut the bird up for placement in the pot. For Suzanna the whole process was the challenge of seeing through something she started, pitting herself against her primal self. She was the victor. Di, however, was transformed in the experience from a woman who tries out everything to an intermediary between two worlds, the Mythic and the mundane. In this process she was changed.

Art

Nowhere is the drama and trauma of rapid social breakdown more publicly portrayed than in the arts. Art reflects life, and life reflects art. A society's lusty exuberance and its sense of peace and harmony are painted, sculpted, danced, expressed in music, and captured in literature. So are its frustrations, pain, and experience of powerlessness. Through these media, ordinary men and women can express themselves powerfully and dramatically without fear of retribution. In the Western world, freedom of artistic expression is one of the most cherished yet threatened values. The arts are still the only *universally* accessible and therefore completely democratic means through which individuals and collectives can speak and be heard. Because the arts reflect the innermost truths of personal and community life, they represent the real pulse of a society. To know a culture or a society is to see it through its creative and imaginal, its mythic self-expression.

The most resilient theme in the arts of postmodern Western culture is the "search for meaning." Sometimes dismissed as "millennium madness," deep personal introspection—with its pain, doubts, and fears—dominates all contemporary Western arts media. Whether it be in the burgeoning industry of New Age and self-help literature, the Rage music of the young, or the stark, graphic drama of dance and theater, the symphony of popular consciousness being played is overwhelmingly passionate disquiet with the state of the world, and the absence or loss of identity and meaning in life. Unsustained by the man-myth of high politics, and its religious zeal for economic rational-ism, people are turning to the Mythic in Celtic, African, and indigenous cultures, to the Goddess cultures of the old world, and to archetypal pantheons of ancient Greece and Rome. Symbols, imagery, and my-thology from the ancient past are being invoked to provide ground-ing, connectedness, and relevance in a spiritually empty, politically uninspiring present. The West is searching for its heart and soul.

For the Ngarinyin, the story is the same, albeit more physically dramatic and direct. They have been physically separated from the land of their being, the place that nourishes their relevance and the mythic life that gives their life its meaning. Notwithstanding this historical fact, Ngarinyin visionaries are seeking to return to their country on the backs of Whitefellas whose search for meaning has brought them to the vast, unexplored, and unexploited galleries of Kimberley rock art. The Lawmen know that the survival of their people is dependent on their being reconnected with their symbols and stories, the ancestral sculptures in the landscape, and the cer-emony and ritual through which they bring meaning and significance to life in song and dance. They recognize that life without a binding collective myth is fragmented and desperate. They witness the wretched emptiness and despair of their people daily in the streets of the towns and fringe camps of urban Australia. They also recognize the similar-ity, if not sameness, in the population of wider Australia, North America, and Europe. Their intention is to bring the Mythic in their arts to the world as a gift, and as a means of their own return to the naming places of their totemic Gi symbols.

Nagomorra Dreaming—the place where Wunggud power is palpable. This is a gallery of Creation and evolution, a place of becoming, paint-layered and engraved in rock walls, sculpted in giant stone forms, citadels, and celebrations of emerging consciousness and cultural continuity from the beginning of time.

As they approached the galleries, Ngarinyin Law dictated that everyone pause while the Lawmen called their invocation to the spirits whose sacred space they entered. "We have students for Bush University. These people from all over Australia, Germany, and America have come to learn about the meaning of land. We are teaching them up in our knowledge. They are our friends."

The children were told to go away from the first gallery. They were not old enough to understand, and not safe from the possible repercussions of ignorant behavior. It was the site where Dumby the Owl had been abused by ignorant children, so their parents and all the adult Ngarinyin tribesmen and tribeswomen were killed. The two young boys who perpetrated the spinifex torture of the Law Owl escaped only to be encased later in the living tomb of an old woman boab tree far away from help. The paintings—transmutations of the episode's characters, and imbued with their spirits—reside in the place where the drama unfolded. Visitations to this hidden gallery activate the subtle energies of their spirits. The story of Dumby is retold. Its meaning for the new world, the new culture of Australia, is poignantly relevant.

The group moved, chastened by the warning of Dumby, to the next gallery. Earlier in the day they had visited a burial cave in the vicinity of a popular Wandjina tourist site. Lawmen Mowaljarlai, Gawanulli, and Neowarra found their ancestors' bones had been scattered by birds. In the presence of Susan, the only Lawwoman there and whose permission was needed to enter the burial area, the group was shown the decorated, oiled, and ochred skulls of the ancients. The enclosed space was cooler, an atmosphere thick with unfamiliar forces. While tourists wandered around beyond the rock enclosure, looking at thousands of years of retouched Wandjina heritage, ignorant of their meaning, significance, and power, the Lawmen conducted their traditional smoking ceremony to be sure the participants did not carry ancestral spirits with them from the area.

Here at Nagomorra, the visitors were again suffused with intangible energies and indescribable powers as Lawmen led them to another secret painting. This was the place that made woman sacred by exposing her essence to adult males who have achieved the maturity to embrace the meaning of divine Mother Woman. Here the Lawmen told the story of male initiation into the mysteries of womanhood. The children and young, uninitiated adolescent boys were again forbidden to view these sacred icons. There is exquisite intimacy in the images—women's vulnerability impaled in ancient rock by timeless artistry, revelation of women's secret self. The women in the group bowed their heads to hide the unrecognized, unexpressed tears of their own deep unknowing.

Just around the corner, obscured by weathering and age, the Law of Wurnan is found written in the images of figurines passing sacred objects to one another in a line that reflects tribal lands from west to east, north to south. Called Guyon Guyon, these predate the ancient Wandjina. They tell the story of early human culture as a reflection of relationship with land. The Guyon Guyon, who gave the tribes ceremony and stone technology, demonstrated the sharing system. All modern kinship and relationship with life was blueprinted tens of thousands of years ago in this small string of elegant images. They are celebrated in a song cycle which foretold human and cultural changes.

Suzanna, whose yearning to conceive a child brought her to Susan the Lawwoman for an increase ritual, was absorbing everything and everyone with her critical legal eye and journalist's microphone. She had been told that something might surrender its life to give her its spirit in the form of a child. She must be alert and fearful for the sign. A little puppy who accompanied the children got in the way of one of the men's feet and unleashed bloodcurdling squeals. Suzanna was horrified. Her fear took over as she sought to check that the puppy was alive, distracted almost to insensibility. Mercifully, it was alive and she returned to her microphone, mindful now that there were powerful subtle energies playing within the group.

Now it was on to the Wunggud Cloud, the single rock massif from which lightning spears the atmosphere, returning in rain and hail, even cyclones. Susan the Lawwoman's grandfather came from this Cloud. Beside it were two pointed stones surrounded by small quartz stones to mark the spirit places, the source of her ancestors just a few generations ago. She had not visited the place for more than thirty years. Overcome with grief and joy at this reunion of souls, Susan and her daughter Jillian enacted their own private smoking. Everyone left them because the intensity of the moment was almost unbearable.

Finally the group came upon the most magnificent Wandjina gallery, at a place whose paintings are called Sweet Water Turtle Dreaming. Images of bubbles gurgled up the cave wall as the turtle sang its sweet song of love. This place celebrates the newest of the human conditions—the sweetness of love and the promise of felicitous union. In awe and reverence, everyone participated in the final smoking of all that had been experienced. They left this holy place, taking with them the stories, signs, vital forces of Creation, and the spirit back to the camp. Once again, they had the sense of being touched by the sacred.

Education

Education is the means by which people learn. Both the curricula *and* the means or method are significant formative influences in the lives of young and old. With the concentration of populations in urban settlements, particularly cities, the design of curricula and the delivery of education in Western culture has become a major, centralized industry. Curricula are designed to fulfill sequential and specifically defined learning outcomes that are able to be measured and standardized across widely dispersed population centers. Knowledge is text based and standardized, and is delivered by academically qualified and specialized teachers and lecturers in specially designated complexes called schools, colleges, and universities. In Western culture, education is devoted to the intellectual development of knowledge and skills. Curricula are designed so that their stated outcomes are measurable. Since only the objective can be measured, subjectivity is discouraged or limited to nonacademic curricula. Western societies are therefore highly intellectual, literate, and numerate, having been grown in the curricula of logos to service the paradigm of Triangle Thinking.

For the Ngarinyin young and old, logos is a complete mystery. Living subjectively in the moment, outside any concept of measured time and space, means that they do not focus on the development of those intellectual skills necessary for theoretical applications. Knowledge is the outcome of guided experiential learning from life, enriched and grounded by the stories, imagery, symbols, and meaning of the Mythic. In following the cycles and patterns of nature, the Ngarinyin receive the world holistically in a spiraling continuum of moments. The outcome is undoubtedly Pattern Thinking—from birth to death, knowledge is never intellectualized or measured. Even their language is verbally photographic and mythic. Each word captures a moment of action that is spoken but not written. Learning is therefore always direct, personal, and interactive.

Few theorists would challenge the premise that experiential learning is generally superior to all other modes; that learning in focus groups rather than as individuals is more valued and valuable; and that practical application of concepts is both easier and more enduring than anything that is theoretically learned. Western students are offered very few opportunities to learn in these ways, or directly from life. The sheer pressure of demand within population concentrations makes this too difficult, if not impossible. Yet this is precisely what many students, parents, and educators seek. It is becoming increasingly apparent that centralized, sedentary, text-based learning is failing to equip people with the life skills, awareness, experience, and knowledge necessary for the health and well-being of themselves and the community. Denied creative social interaction because of the increasing pressure and rigor of text-based learning that has now infiltrated family and leisure time, adolescents are becoming less able to deal with ordinary emotional and social challenges that living in community, and relationships, inevitably raise. For some parents, home-based education has become a preferred option for their children. Others are working as collectives to offer their young people so-called alternative education which usually incorporates the principle of "learning *from* life" rather than the centralized system that applies the principle "learning *about* life."

The elder Ngarinyin Lawmen know that the three generations that follow them probably have been too damaged to incorporate Western values with any real competence. They are often spiritually lost because they have borne the brunt of Western policies of assimilation and integration and been denied access to the older people in the Law. As a result, they recognize that if the young generation of children are to grow grounded in their lives, they must come to terms with Western culture, and learn Western competencies and skills. At the same time, they continue to go through the old Law so they can then use these Western skills to maintain Ngarinyin culture. The Lawmen also acknowledge that they have an educational experience that would greatly enhance the development of school students in the Western system. They recognize that, like their own young people,

Western children seem lost, empty inside, without meaning in their lives. Like many concerned Western parents, the Ngarinyin realize that neither Pattern Thinking nor Triangle Thinking alone prepares or equips the young for their inevitable future.

I am an old man now, and want to tell you this.

I grew up in Kunmunya Mission, far away from European civilization. My father and mother were full tribal, in the Law, and I was born in the Earth, proper way. Mr. Love, the Presbyterian Mission Superintendent, was a really good man. He did not try to destroy our tribal Law and culture. He encouraged my people to stay in the Law, and to continue teaching the young ones the tribal way of life. I grew up in the Law, bush way, the old way. I also learned to read and write in the Mission because Mr. Love said to my father, "Mowaljarlai will have many problems in his lifetime. He will have to live in two worlds, Whitefella and Blackfella. He must be able to read Whitefella milli milli (documents)." I really appreciated Mr. Love.

Since that time I have seen my Ngarinyin people nearly destroyed by European culture and settlement. In just two generations of time, I have witnessed four generations of my people die off too young, have early heart attacks, or get brain dead from alcohol and despair. Many of my people are lost to themselves, lost to the Law, and lost to Australian society. Every day we Lawmen cry for our people, especially for our young ones coming up. "What future do they have?" we say. "We Ngarinyin have not benefited from our relationship with Whitefellas. For all the government money and policies, we are not better off—we are worse off."

We old Lawmen are doing something about this now, before it is too late. We have to prepare the way for our young people, our young girls and boys. We have to get them out of the despair and destruction of the towns and settlements before they get caught by alcohol, anger, and death.

We have decided to send our children out, away from us for their youthful years. We are establishing our Bush University and our Ngarinyin Culture College for them to return to when they come home.

I have come to Guildford Grammar School for my two young boys, Claude and Gideon, because you have been supporting Aboriginal people.

In my culture, when boys reach the age of puberty, they are handed over to older men, not father, for their manhood training. In our Law the young boys have to be trained a special, male way so they grow up to be strong, stable, responsible men. This is their rites of passage, their destiny.

They are separated from girls during this time of their lives. It is a very hard time for them. They have to learn responsibility, courage, endurance, obedience in the Law, self-discipline, and skills in hunting, ceremony and ritual, painting, song, dance, and the meaning of life, represented in our stories and evidence in the country. They must learn the proper way to behave with elders, women, nature, and the Earth. They have to be trained in their spirituality and understanding of the meaning of life. This way they learn to know who they are, what is their identity, and what is their belonging. We call this "learning for life." That is the name we have given our Bush University experience.

The four generations of our people that have been damaged by European culture are the people who should be training our young men and women. They are not there for them. So now we are looking to European culture to do this in partnership with us.

Guildford Grammar School offers what our people cannot provide in this generation. For our Lawmen, it is right that your school is all boys from puberty. It is right that there are older men (and women) other than father to teach and guide them as they mature. It is right that you have a strong spiritual foundation which soaks through all of their learning life. You teach respect for elders, women, nature, and the Earth. You provide training in responsibility, obedience in the Law, courage, and endurance. The boys will learn self-discipline. You navigate boys into full, strong manhood, proud and fearless, respectful and submissive. This is what we do in our culture because this is the right way in the Law.

We think the way of the future is Two-Way Thinking. Two cultures sharing the responsibility of training all of our young people. We want to offer you the opportunity to send your boys up to us Ngarinyin

Lawmen in our country so we can train them in the meaning of land, of life, the evidence in the country, the spirituality of this continent, Men's Business, and becoming full-bodied, strong men. We want to talk about a partnership in education for your young men and for ours. The future depends on young men and women being trained properly with strong values and traditions in both our cultures because you and we are the people of Australia—the original people and the new culture. Our future must be two cultures, two ways, working together.

This is why I came to Guildford Grammar—because it is strong in the same values and traditions as Ngarinyin culture. We have this opportunity to work together, for all of our young people.

DAVID MOWALJARLAI, OAM, Ngarinyin Lawman
in a letter to the headmaster of Guildford Grammar School
Perth, Western Australia, 1996

Just twenty-four hours after the new boys returned from hunting and gathering their designer-label clothing and equipment I visited the Ngarinyin boys. I told them that we were not taking them to the cities tonight because of the incident during the week involving the stash of clothes, Walkmans, and CDs that they had collected and bagged to take to Mowanjum. I came home to relax.

When the telephone rang at 10.30 P.M. my heart sank. The housemaster of their boardinghouse is the only person who rings me late at night. "They've done a flit. They're gone," he said, laconically now, rather than with outrage, nervousness, or despair.

I felt powerless. Ranging through my knowledge, drawing on my meager wisdom I pondered the dimensions of the problem, asking myself, "How do we reach them? How do we connect with their morality, responsibility, accountability, obedience? How can we assert our authority? If the headmaster's authority is ignored, and the housemaster's authority is ignored, and my authority is cast aside, what on Earth can any of us do? Is the Ngarinyin Initiative a dream unfulfillable, however altruistic its intent?" Drifting into uneasy sleep in the wee small hours I handed the issue over to Wunggud, God, and history.

Early on Saturday morning I rang their father. "Ah, good! You rang. There is something I want to talk to you about, but what did you ring me for?" he said. I told him that the boys had broken bounds despite the full weight of all of our individual and collective authority. We were not reaching them, I told him. The boys were just not respecting our rules and laws. It was as if they were rendering us and our rules of law invisible. They were roaming free in the city without any sense of accountability. "They are not respecting us," I said. "If we do not have their respect, we are powerless to train them as you have asked."

I then told him of my night's inner struggle. Two of the boys have no relationship experience with Whitefellas, I began. Their only exposure to Whitefellas has been with the police and schoolteachers. They have no real knowledge or awareness of how our culture operates, what constitutes our authority system or any other social system, and no knowledge of protocols, beliefs, attitudes, values, or customary behaviors. The only authority they know and respect is their own Ngarinyin system. They only really listen to the Lawmen, and other kinship authority. In Perth, this internal and external system of checks and balances was, and is, absent. So they feel they are free of boundaries, rules, and law. Our system is invisible to them not because they are naughty or defiant but because they are ignorant.

The old Lawman listened without interruption, without comment. I told him we cannot allow the boys to be endangered or damaged by their experience here so they would have to return home, or a Lawman would have to come to the city to bridge the authority gap, to explain and relate our authority to their own, to navigate them with us, and to teach them that they do not know what they do not know.

The old man then closed the subject of the boys, and turned to his own subject. He said, "I want to talk to you about this land business. You know, all this talk about extinguishing Native Title, about rights—Whitefella and Blackfella—they still not listening. We've been telling them for a hundred million years about this business—the Seamen inquiry, anthropologists, scientists, lawyers, everybody all the time. Somebody new comes to work in our country and they ring us up and ask us all these questions about who we are in the land. Everybody new wants to hear our story all over again. We are tired of telling them over and over. How come they don't know by now? Now there's this new decision, and the government is trying to extinguish our title. They still don't recognize our authority. They're still ignorant of our Law.

"We have to teach them gently about our Gi symbols in the land. We have to teach them more that every bird, every emu, every frog, and tree, they are all our relations, our grandmothers, and fathers, and uncles. This is what they extinguish. How come they don't listen to us? How come they don't respect our authority about Aborigine culture? How come they don't see us? They make up their own rules about how to behave in our land. We are powerless now. We don't really know what to do because they do not respect us and our Law.

"We must teach them about our Gi symbols, who we are, and about our Law. We gotta teach them they can't extinguish Native Title because they extinguish all our families."

The conversation ended.

The insight exploded in my head. As I went through the issues again in my mind, I could see that we are now experiencing exactly what the Ngarinyin are experiencing in their relationship with Whitefellas and our culture. They struggle with the fact that archeologists, tourists, other researchers, or the simply curious roam around their country without guidance and without permission because they don't know any better. They are ignorant of the authority of the Ngarinyin Lawmen, so fail to acknowledge it. Sacred objects—rocks, images, stone tools—are taken out of Ngarinyin country to be put in suburbia on a museum shelf or a domestic mantlepiece. Just like the stash the boys were collecting—our sacred objects of money and possessions!

The transition from the bush to boarding needs to be carefully and sensitively staged so the Ngarinyin students are not pushed beyond their ability to absorb the new culture, its way of seeing, its beliefs, values, and expectations. At the same time we must take our own teachers through the values and beliefs of Ngarinyin culture so that our decisions and programs are based on Two-Way awareness rather than superimposed in ignorance. We have the opportunity to arrest our culture's psychosocial extinguishment of tribal culture by meeting the challenge the Ngarinyin offer us as they entrust their children to our care.

I believe we now have an approach to this challenge which gives the Ngarinyin Initiative a shape for which we can effectively prepare strategies. We now need to simply acknowledge the assumptions, recognize the behaviors, and deduce the gaps and ravines of cultural ignorance *in ourselves and in our culture's historic and contemporary interaction with the original culture,* to design pathways for the boys (and hopefully girls) who will come to us for cocultural education. This is the story of "Reflections." We and the Ngarinyin are faced with exactly the same challenges based on the same experiences, mirrored in each other in the present.

HANNAH RACHEL BELL
in a letter to the headmaster of Guildford Grammar School, 1997

Western and indigenous cultures have a great deal to learn from each other. Both cultures are in a stage of transition of millennial significance.

Primary Aboriginal culture, experienced and literally lived in the Mythic, is disappearing off the face of the Earth, dying out with its oldest tribal Lawmen and Lawwomen. The Ngarinyin visionaries who are still fully in the old Law have dedicated their last years to preserving their knowledge in forms that are readily accessible to the rest of the world. This in itself is a quantum leap for them because, until the last decade, Ngarinyin and other Aboriginal tribes had remained within their own Wurnan systems, closed to participation in the affairs of state beyond their own specific totemic and linguistic boundaries. This represents a profound step into the future, one that no tribes have taken in many thousands of years, and that they do now only because they hear their death knell ringing. The Ngarinyin are not the only Aboriginal people on this new journey. All over Australia, tribal people are painting their mythologies and symbols on transportable materials and in new media. They are not doing this traditionally, not as an integral part of a particular ritual or ceremony but for the world to experience in all its culturally diverse spaces. Several tribes have developed tourism experiences that invite outsiders into the heart and soul of their culture.

The Ngarinyin have embarked on a comprehensive vision for the future, in partnership with visionary Whitefellas, that is based on the philosophy of Two-Way Thinking. Their initiatives include cocultural film, art, and books that invite the world into their symbols and meaning, to personally absorb and collectively share. They are simultaneously establishing enduring initiatives for direct, cultural educational exchanges with specific institutions and with the world at large. Their nagging problem, however, is their historic dispossession from land, and the tardiness of political processes to redress this. For as long as they do not have legal title to their country, their access to the land that names them, in which all of their cultural knowledge, Law, and meaning abide, is threatened. They are therefore prevented from consolidating their vision in concrete form.

For some time now the Ngarinyin have been attempting to have their Wandjina landscape, a discrete geographic subregion of the remote Kimberley, protected as a sanctuary of the living Mythic for the world's access and inheritance. This mostly pristine wilderness encompasses the tableland headwaters of seven river systems, plateaux, gorges, strings of waterholes, and the Wandjina galleries. It represents the most powerful living cultural museum of the history of humanity anywhere on Earth. Threatened by the possibility of extractive industries, popular market tourism, and new, experimental land uses, the Ngarinyin are desperate to achieve the respect necessary for their culture's physical iconography, energetic systems, Law, and knowledge to be preserved and protected for the next millennium's societies.

The Western world is starting to experience the death throes of its own unsustainable ethos. Having become separated from the myth that sustained it for two millennia, Western culture's political leadership continues to opt for its own man-managed and changeable myths whose bottom line is currently economic rationalism. The fact that broad-based social change is happening is unquestioned. The millennial changes that Western societies are experiencing are not being initiated by their democratically elected political leaders but by their citizenry. People are withdrawing their respect for, and participation in, the ideologies and systems that are designed to control and suppress their instinctual drives and knowledge.

Not since Greek and Roman times has there been such a profound, fundamental shake-up in the evolution of the ethos of Western man. As more people turn to the Mythic in the cultural heritage of the Celts, Greeks, Romans, and the original cultures on Earth, the search for meaning becomes a pathway in its own right. As demonstrated by the Ngarinyin and other culturally ancient Aboriginal peoples, the quantum leap in consciousness that they are experiencing is upon us all.

Joseph Campbell once said, "There are four faces to fulfilling human potential. These are: one, acknowledge all 'signs' because this is the way the Earth speaks; two, embrace 'chance' as holding a meaning just for you, because this is the way life speaks; three, listen mindfully to the 'inner voice,' because this is the way wisdom speaks; and four, follow your bliss."

I thought I knew this in 1990 but it took a deep dive into the depression of frustrated anger and a trip to the Kimberley to realize the experience of these words. I visited my longtime friend, Ngarinyin Lawman David Mowaljarlai, in Derby and we went to the May River for a picnic. As we explored ways of ensuring that the next generation of Ngarinyin receive their culture's knowledge, wisdom, and processes, we ate apples, then threw the cores into the river. We watched them in silence. Instead of catching the strong current on the other side, both cores turned around and came back to us, caught in an eddy. I felt strangely disturbed at this and commented to Mowaljarlai, "That's a bit like you and me right now—it could be we are stuck in an eddy." He agreed.

I wanted my core to go into the main current rather than continuing to float around sluggishly in the backwater. Mowaljarlai was caught up in the feeling too. We followed their progress with all-consuming attention. Around they went again, sometimes one lagging behind the other, then catching up, then bumping into each other, then passing. Around they went for a third time.

At last my core jumped over the eddy's edge, caught the current and swirled off toward the rapids, over them, and beyond our sight. Mowaljarlai's core came back again. He picked up some rocks and threw them near the core, attempting to make bow waves to push it into the current. The river seemed to change color and a thunderstorm grew behind us, blanketing us with its eerie darkness. He asked me to help throw rocks toward his core, but around it went again. By now he was blind to everything else. He was almost desperate to get his core into the vigorous part of the river.

After several more journeys in the eddy, it finally jumped over. Happy and relieved he looked up to see a hawk swoop low over the river and us. The thunderstorm skirted us without striking, leaving a trail of brilliance. Mowaljarlai smiled and said, "You have to help us tell our story."

Christina Kennedy

Claude Mowaljarlai in the art room at Guildford Grammar School.

Postscript

Two-Way Thinking is more than simply a name conjured to describe two cultures working respectfully and cooperatively together. It challenges a fundamental assumption of Western culture, in which its intellectual tradition is rooted. The assumption is that the sophisticated number and word language systems of modern civilizations represent the only legitimate tools by which humans can describe, synthesize, and therefore comprehend the world around them. The nationwide network of dedicated Whitefellas called Friends of the Ngarinyin, who are privileged to enjoy friendship and work with Ngarinyin elders and young people, are slowly realizing that the Ngarinyin synthesize experience and information in a different way. This has become evident in all the cocultural projects in which they collaborate, but it is most evident to the educators of the young Ngarinyin who are participants in the cocultural education initiative.

There are currently ten Ngarinyin students enrolled in five schools and colleges three-thousand kilometers away from their Kimberley region homelands. They have been granted Mowaljarlai Memorial Scholarships with the requirement that they and their parents participate fully in the program, which includes student education in private colleges in Perth, Western Australia, socialization in the homes and families of their new friends and classmates, sharing their cultural knowledge and experience within the schools and the wider community, and hosting Bush University visits by Western students. The scholarships are granted to students whose families continue to live within the philosophy of their traditional law, and whose access to specialist educational and recreational opportunities is limited.

The Ngarinyin Educational Initiative began in 1995 with just two boys, supported by one college, and a small group of volunteer women who assisted me in looking after them on weekends, attending their sporting events, assisting in communication and understanding of the boys' thinking and behavior, providing pocket money and clothing, and attending to their health and recreational needs. When the boys returned to their community in the Kimberley for school holidays the elders were pleased with their progress, and many mothers contacted us to ask if their sons and daughters could also come to Perth for their education. At that point I enlisted the support of the Anglican archbishop of Perth, Dr. Peter Carnley, who, after meeting with the elders, agreed to take a significant personal and pastoral interest in the students and their families. He attended Bush University, got involved in the ordinary lives of the Ngarinyin families, took over financial sponsorship of the noneducational aspects of the Initiative, provided a large, permanent city base camp for the Ngarinyin elders and students, started a cocultural education foundation, and personally welcomed eight more students in the subsequent two years.

In 1998 two groups of students traveled to the Kimberley to attend Bush University. The colleges, which provide first-class education for their students, soon realized that much of the curricula and standard teaching methodologies were in many ways inadequate, in that they failed to respond to the way in which the Ngarinyin students synthesize experience and information. Special tutoring was immediately coordinated by Swanleigh Residential College, where all the Ngarinyin students reside. The College's Director, Allan Meney, a keen and innovative educator with a history of developing creative responses to youth issues, took up the challenge to develop an effective teaching paradigm that responds to the visual/spatial thinking style of the

Ngarinyin students. He is supported by the head of John Septimus Roe Anglican Community School, Matthew Hughes, who has committed staff resources to the pastoral care of the students and to initiating an "in field" response whereby a staff member would stay with the Ngarinyin in their country to better understand the cultural and natural influences that shape their hearts and minds.

The Ngarinyin and the Friends of the Ngarinyin are unable to predict whether the Initiative will be successful or not, or to even define what success might be. All we really know is that to continue to do nothing about the gross ignorance of Aboriginal law and culture within all levels of Australian society, and to continue to ignore the dismal lack of social and educational opportunities for remote and traditional Aboriginal people, is tantamount to civic neglect of unparalleled proportions. The Ngarinyin elders and the Friends are bonded in a long-term commitment to travel the pathway together, and to address the challenges as they arise.

Aboriginal land rights continues to be one of the most socially divisive and culturally inequitable issues facing Australians. While Aboriginal rights to land were recognized by the Australian federal government as far back as 1976, and the High Court of Australia affirmed in 1992 that preexisting Native Title is a reality that must be recognized by the national parliament, every significant step toward its recognition has been thwarted by powerful vested interests, bigoted political lobbyists, and uninformed popular resistance and fear. Legislation passed by the federal parliament in 1998 rendered Native Title economically insubstantial and politically powerless, and represents little more than a gesture of recognition which is devoid of real knowledge or respect. The Friends of the Ngarinyin, who include church leaders, doctors, retired judges, writers, broadcasters, business people, filmmakers, and publishers, are committed to ensuring that the Wandjina cultural heritage, rock art, lands, and tribes are protected from further desecration. To this end the Friends' network, in conjunction with Ngarinyin elders, is establishing a foundation that will own land according to Australian law and is assisting in negotiations for the purchase of those traditional lands where the seriously endangered Wandjina galleries are unprotected from ignorant and exploitative non-Aboriginal access and abuse. These highly vulnerable lands hold the entire history of continuous human culture on Earth in the rock art, and are in great peril of destruction by Western economic land uses such as unfettered ranching and mining. Their preservation is considered of paramount importance not only for the Ngarinyin, Worrora, and Wanumbal peoples, who are the direct, continuous inheritors of this sacred law, but for all of humanity. It is our own human heritage, with the visually recorded history of human consciousness that is evident within the Wandjina galleries, that in a sense provides us all with the awareness of our human roots.

For many years the Ngarinyin have sought to conduct their political, social, economic, and cultural business independently of governments and pan-Aboriginal political organizations who are financed by, and are therefore accountable to, governments. It continues to be quite a struggle because the nationally structured and funded regional Aboriginal councils are very powerful. Under their independent flagship organization Kamali Council, originally established to represent the interests of the three Wandjina tribes, the Ngarinyin initiated the Ngarinyin Aboriginal Corporation and the Ngarinyin Culture College, the latter being the organization that controls Bush University. In recent times many Worrora and Wanumbal people have rekindled their interest and participation in the activities of Kamali and once again have joined forces to conduct Bush University and to develop a major art project to finance their cultural and economic survival. Tribal Lawmen and Lawwomen from everywhere in the Wandjina lands are painting canvases of their country, their Gi animals and plants, and the Wunggud places which name them and give them their identity. In the process the elders are teaching their younger kinspeople the ancient arts and stories. The paintings are then recorded as evidence of their relationship in the land, and constitute a comprehensive visual, iconographic legal testimony. The sale and lease of the paintings generates revenue to support the operational costs of Kamali Council and cultural events, and the costs of running their Native Title and other legal cases.

In 1997 the Ngarinyin, in partnership with filmmaker Jeff Doring's Pathways Project, presented sacred, previously unseen evidence to the UNESCO organization in Paris. The elders who accompanied Doring to the UNESCO forum, organized specifically to receive their ancient knowledge, later traveled to the famous Lascaux caves in southern France to view the oldest paintings in the Northern Hemisphere. Here the elders were able to bring new understanding and insight to some of the icons and symbols in the gallery and, to the great surprise and delight of the professionals and academics studying there, gave a spontaneous demonstration of manufacturing a stone spear point. The significance of the demonstration was immense. The academics realized, as did all witnesses to the exercise, that these contemporary lawmen held stone tool manufacturing knowledge that had disappeared from the Northern Hemisphere perhaps ten thousand years ago. Pathways Project film, photographs, and sound recordings are now being cataloged and produced for international distribution. Already the project's influence is being seen in the formal renaming by Australian universities of a very early art form, formerly known as the Bradshaw paintings, to the Ngarinyin name of Guyon Guyon.

Bush University remains the centerpiece of all the Ngarinyin and Friends' cocultural initiatives because it is the direct experience of stepping through the dimension of time from a linear, constructed present into the timeless Mythic, the Dreaming. In Bush University generations of Blackfellas and Whitefellas share lives and stories around the campfires, sitting amongst bedding, animals, killed bush turkey, or kangaroo on the backs of trucks, swimming in the sacred Wunggud waterholes, fishing, hunting, sharing Men's Business and Women's Business with each other. Bush University is accessible to anyone from anywhere in the world who is able to make the considerable investment of time and money to travel to this extremely remote part of the planet. Most who attend become a Friend of the Ngarinyin and subsequently enjoy the fraternity and communication made possible by global digital technology. The next step is to make the rest of the world and the Wandjina tribes accessible to each other, using the same sophisticated communication systems that are currently being used by nations and corporations to generate unprecedented globalization in world affairs.

Throughout his last season of Bush University Mowaljarlai focused on the theme of Death. It was as if he was responding to a premonition of his own passing, because he made sure that everyone with whom he came in contact was aware that he wanted his final passage to be the traditional, tribal rite to ensure the certainty of his own journey to Dulugun. Prior to the last Bush University tour of 1997 one of his sons died in tragic circumstances while in police custody. As Mowaljarlai finished off the last trip he grieved openly for this son, surrounded by the Whitefellas whom he had been teaching. Coincidentally perhaps, the biggest recorded earthquake struck the Kimberley at this time. Its epicenter was in the islands just off the Kimberley coast in the Ngarinyin Land of the Dead, or Dulugun. Its reach radiated throughout the Wandjina lands. Mowaljarlai's son was buried in the Derby cemetery after a Christian funeral rite. Mowaljarlai became quite emphatic that, when he himself died, he did not want to be buried in the ground where his spirit would be locked up. He wanted his bones and spirit to join those of his ancestors, in the rock shelter of his Wunggud spirit.

When Mowaljarlai died two weeks after his son's burial Whitefellas and Blackfellas alike worked feverishly to give him his final wish. Western Australian laws relating to disposal of the deceased had to be suspended by political intervention with ministerial dispensation to enable the Old Man's body to be laid out in the traditional manner. The nonsectarian yet religious funeral service was conducted by Father Frank Brennan, a Jesuit priest who had been deeply involved in social justice and Native Title issues. It was an inspirational, cocultural event incorporating ancient and modern Aboriginal and Western ceremonies, performed by Mowaljarlai's Western friends and Aboriginal kin. His body was then flown out to his country where he was traditionally laid out on a death platform by his Ngarinyin relations. As in his life, Mowaljarlai challenged all those who knew him to reflect Two-Way Thinking in his final rite of passage.

Further information about the Wandjina tribes, the Friends of the Ngarinyin, and their projects is available by e-mail at narinyin@omen.net.au or from The Friends of the Ngarinyin, Post Office Gidgegannup, Western Australia 6083.